TAMING

NARCISSISM

TOXIC

NONSENSE

EGOS

REBECCA P FOX

This edition first published in paperback by
Michael Terence Publishing in 2023
www.mtp.agency

ISBN 9781800945692

Michael Terence
Publishing

What to Expect

This book teaches you how to spot, deal with and successfully live in a world full of narcissists, also known as incredibly big toxic egos. It's no surprise that in today's world so many people are becoming obsessed with getting validation from strangers on the internet. And let's face it, getting likes and positive comments from others does give us a boost, but has this obsession become the prevalent cause of narcissism? And, more importantly, how can you deal with those who suffer from big and rather toxic egos?

In this book, psychotherapist Rebecca P Fox talks you through how to deal with all narcissists. You will develop a level of understanding around how a narcissist is created, what impact they have on our society and the mental and emotional health of those they come in contact with. This book will provide you with the blueprint for the five most common types of narcissists that you come across every day, including those who simply have a few narcissistic traits but are still rather difficult to put up with. You will learn where narcissism comes from and how you can stop it from becoming a toxic set of traits.

All narcissists have the same things in common: they all have inflated egos that crave praise, admiration and have zero empathy. Narcissists navigate the world with a sense of self-importance and they fantasise about success and grandeur. However, don't be fooled into thinking that all narcissists are the same. In fact, there are five subtypes who have very distinctive *modi operandi*. By taking a closer look at different types of narcissists, you will be able to understand the way these master manipulators work and the reason behind everything they do.

While there is no cure for narcissism, there certainly is a remedy for the way we approach and deal with those suffering from unusually big, inflated egos; it's called emotional intelligence.

When you unlock a higher level of emotional intelligence, narcissists will no longer be able to dominate your life. And even if you happen to come across one, be it on the bus, at work or on a dating app, they simply won't stick around long enough to make your life miserable when they realise they have no power over you. Don't forget *what does not kill us, makes us stronger.* Once you learn how to make the most out of the big toxic egos you encounter, you might even find yourself looking forward to taking on the next narcissist who crosses your path.

About the Author

Rebecca P Fox is a UK-based psychotherapist and emotional intelligence consultant who has formulated a unique rewiring method that uses a mixture of behavioural therapies and pattern disruption to help people heal from trauma. She is no stranger to trauma herself. Having been raised in a loveless family dynamic with a difficult narcissistic mother, Rebecca developed numerous mental and emotional health conditions that turned her into a very anxious, unhappy child. She then fell into the arms of a violent narcissistic boyfriend, as do many who have an abusive childhood. He continued to add to her trauma and lack of self-worth with daily abuse. The relationship was a violent one, and it was the last physical attack by him which proved the turning point in Rebecca's life.

After waking up in hospital in a bloody state, she was made aware of the support available which could enable her to leave the abusive boyfriend and have the possibility of starting anew. So, she did, but the recovery was a long and costly one. Rebecca went through years of therapy with various practitioners to deal with the trauma she had experienced during her childhood and violent relationship. She was an unconfident, high-functioning stress addict who never understood the 'point' of life. She felt awkward in social situations, had difficulty forming friendships and relationships and trusted no one; so, putting her trust in a therapist was difficult. The hardest part for her was that no one seemed to understand how she felt or how her experiences had affected her.

After studying psychology, personality disorders and trauma in particular, she gained numerous qualifications and began to understand what she was subjected to wasn't because of who she was as a person, which had been her belief for many years. Instead, the trauma she experienced was a result of the 'types' of people she was surrounded by. Since then, she has completely changed her life and become unrecognisable from the person she once was. She is dedicated to helping others overcome their trauma so they can live full, authentic lives.

Dedications

Frances Ann McCaffrey
31st October 1959 - 26th September 2021

In Loving Memory of Frances Ann McCaffrey,
Whose untimely passing left an indelible mark on our hearts.
Your unwavering love and friendship lifted us up,
And your legacy lives on in the memories we cherish.

To my dear Frances,
You broke my heart and your passing pushed me to grow,
And I'm forever grateful for the impact you had on my life.
Your memory will always inspire me to strive for greatness,
And I will carry your love with me forever.

For Frances,
Your spirit shines bright in the lives you touched,
And your light will never fade.
Your body may be gone, but your beautiful memory lives on,
In the hearts of all those who loved and cherished you.

Rest in peace, Frances Ann McCaffrey.
Forever in our hearts, forever in our thoughts.

Contents

1: Why Narcissists are the Way they Are 1
- Childhood experiences
- Parenting styles
- Can a child be diagnosed as a 'narcissist' early on and can it be prevented?
- Narcissistic cultures

2: Social Media and Narcissism 17
- Contributing factors
- The impact social media documentation has on a child's mental and emotional health

3: Am I a Narcissist? 23
- Emotional and cognitive empathy
- The narcissistic spectrum
- Clickbait
- Sadism

4: How to Spot a Narcissist 36
- Narcissistic Personality Disorder
- Narcissistic supply
- NPD subtypes
- Narcissistic patterns
- Cognitive dissonance
- Communication styles

5: The Narcissist's Toolbox 46
- Emotional manipulation
- Gaslighting types
- Belittling
- Blaming and shaming
- Silent treatment
- Manipulation
- Intermittent reinforcement
- Blocking and ghosting
- Triangulation
- Projection

6: Type One: The Ultimate Narcissist 64
- Signs of a grandiose narcissist
- Social media influence

7: Type Two: Covert Narcissist – aka the Victim 70
- Signs of a covert narcissist
- Passive aggression

8: Type Three: Communal Narcissist – aka the Hero 76
- Signs of a communal narcissist
- Suitable job roles

9: Type Four: Malignant Narcissist – the Quintessence of Evil 81
- Signs of a malignant narcissist
- Antisocial behaviour
- Reactive abuse

10: Type Five: Seductive – aka the Euphoric Narcissist 88
- Signs of a sexual narcissist
- Sexual addiction
- Narcissists love triangle

11: Why Victims Feel Stuck 98
- Trauma bonds
- Smear campaigns
- Flying monkeys
- Triggers

12: How to Handle a Partner with a Big Ego 110
- Grey rocking
- No contact

13: How to Handle Narcissistic Families 115
- Narcissistic family dynamics
- Narcissistic parents
- Narcissistic siblings
- Narcissistic adult children
- Yellow rocking

14: How to Handle a Friend with a Big Ego 124
- Jealousy

15: How to Handle Big Egos at Work ... 127
- Dark triad
- Narcissism
- Machiavellianism
- Psychopathy
- Processes to deal with a narcissistic work colleague

16: Emotional Intelligence: the Game Changer ... 140
- Emotional intelligence development
- Self-perception/awareness
- Self-expression
- Interpersonal
- Decision making
- Stress management

17: How to Deal with a Narcissist – Once and for All ... 157
- Boundaries
- Values
- Values exercise
- Standards

Values Table ... 172

References ... 173

1

Why Narcissists are the Way they Are

This is a question I get asked the most, and it is one of those questions that unfortunately I am not able to give a definite answer to. However, I am yet to meet someone who hasn't dated a narcissist that claims they had a difficult, abusive childhood. While narcissists tend not to use this statement as an excuse for their behaviour, it does seem to be a common thread for those who are difficult and narcissistic, which ties into what we do know about why narcissists are the way they are, and it comes down to these four factors:

Childhood experiences:
Narcissistic traits can develop in response to early childhood experiences, such as neglect, emotional abuse or overindulgence. A child who is constantly criticised or made to feel inadequate, may develop a sense of grandiosity or entitlement as a way to compensate.

Genetics:
Some research suggests that certain genetic factors may contribute to the development of narcissistic personality traits. Studies have found that there may be a hereditary component to narcissism, although the exact mechanisms are not well understood.

Cultural influences:
Cultural values that emphasise individualism, competition and success may contribute to the development of narcissistic traits. In some cultures, narcissistic behaviour may be seen as a sign of strength or success, rather than as a negative trait.

Neurological factors:
Some research has suggested that differences in brain structure or function may contribute to the development of narcissism. For example, studies have found that people with narcissistic traits may have reduced activity in brain regions associated with empathy and self-reflection.

Let's start by looking deeper into how childhood experiences impact narcissism.

It is normal and healthy for a child to have a sense of self-importance and self-confidence. When a child is well-adjusted and has a healthy self-esteem, they are able to understand they are not the centre of the universe and the feelings and needs of others are just as important as their own.

Children always want attention, and as babies they need the world to revolve around them with their needs getting met on a consistent basis. Usually as they get older, they become less needy and their selfish ways become more transparent. This shift doesn't mean that a child will become a narcissist because they no longer demand your attention and have started to take care of their own needs. It just means that they are growing up, finding their independence and learning how to navigate the world.

Narcissism is not considered to be an important part of a healthy child's development. In fact, excessive levels of narcissism can be harmful to a child's social and emotional development. Narcissistic traits, such as an inflated sense of self-importance and a lack of empathy, can make it difficult for a child to form healthy relationships with others and to understand the perspectives and feelings of those around them.

When certain traits and behaviours that are associated with narcissism are present in children and adolescents, it is important to pay attention to them. A child cannot be diagnosed as a narcissist, as not all children who show these traits will develop a disorder. It is important to recognise that the development of a personality disorder is a complex process, and it is influenced by many factors.

Our childhood is a time when our mental and emotional universe is wide open.

In the early years of their life children only absorb emotions, meaning they don't fully understand them. It is down to their caregivers and peers to help them properly navigate their mental and emotional worlds. It is the early years of our lives where we are shaped as humans, and this is also when narcissistic traits are programmed into a person's behavioural repertoire.

Some experts argue that narcissism is hereditary, as some children seem to be mirror images of their narcissistic parents. Now I fully understand this theory because that is what some of the evidence suggests, however, not all children will turn out to be just like their narcissistic parents.

Temperament plays a role in a child's personality type; it is known that those with over sensitive temperaments are more at risk of developing narcissistic traits. Children do instinctively want to learn from those they love, and they want to please those they love. So, if they are shown a particular way to behave in order to get noticed this becomes a way for life for them. This behaviour is called *mirroring*, it's a natural behaviour that a child does to develop a bond with their parents.

While no child is perfect, when a child is showing difficult behaviours, there could be many reasons for this. Often children will act out because they are confused, anxious, tired and feel hurt. This acting out can often get misinterpreted with the child being classed as a narcissist. Some traits of narcissism are a normal part of a child's development. Understanding these traits and to which level is important.

While it is difficult to confirm the exact cause of narcissism, the development of narcissism is firmly impacted by the environment in which the child is raised. The environment is likely to be a toxic one, where the parents or caregivers neglect the child's emotional needs.

Here are some key factors that can contribute to a child developing narcissism:

- **Overindulgent parenting style**
  – spoiling the child

We all want to give our children the things we never had growing up and more! It is normal to want to see our children happy and fulfilled. However, children who are spoiled and given everything they want, will grow up believing that they are entitled to whatever they want. Spoilt children learn they don't have to work for, or earn anything, and they are given what they want just for existing.

Physical items then become a way of defining their worth. This is also the time when a materialistic belief is likely to be developed, this belief aligns with their sense of worth which develops into extreme entitlement that is associated with narcissism.

Additionally, children who are raised by overindulgent parents are not provided with structure and boundaries. They will likely struggle with impulse control, and may engage in risky or inappropriate behaviour. This is because overindulgent parents do not enforce rules and boundaries. As a result, the children then make up their own rules which always tend to go in their favour. 'No' is something they are not used to hearing so they don't know what it is like to be disappointed. Children who are raised by overindulgent parents have difficulty managing their emotions because they have not yet learned how to cope with disappointment and frustration.

Many people have a belief that those who had everything growing up were lucky, and had nothing to moan about. But usually, this overindulged lifestyle would come at a cost.

That cost was having absent parents. This absence wasn't always intentional, often it would be due to work reasons, and the 'spoiling' behaviour was a way to compensate their child for not always being there. This would result in an emotional disconnect.

- **Helicopter parenting**
  – Stripping away independence

Helicopter parenting is characterised by parents who are overly involved in their child's life and make decisions for them, rather than allowing the child to make their own choices and learn from their mistakes. The parent is the one who becomes the 'brains' for that child.

This style of parenting can have a number of negative effects on a child's mental and emotional growth. For example, children who are overindulged will have difficulty developing a sense of self, as they have not had the opportunity to make their own decisions and learn from their mistakes. They may also struggle with independence and decision making, as they are used to having their parents make decisions for them.

Additionally, children who are raised in this way may have difficulty coping with failure, and may become overly reliant on their parents. They may also experience anxiety and depression and have difficulty forming healthy relationships with their peers.

In order for children to develop healthy mental and emotional growth, it is important for parents to provide structure and guidance while also allowing children to make their own decisions, learn from their mistakes and take responsibility for their actions. This can involve setting boundaries, being consistent with discipline, and encouraging children to take on age-appropriate responsibilities.

Children who are raised in this 'helicopter' style will struggle with independence, making decisions will feel like an impossible task for them, and they will have difficulty coping with failure, leading to anxiety, depression and difficulty forming relationships.

- **Parents putting their needs before their child's**
  – neglectful parenting style

Children are born with a need to look for love and affection from their parents. When they are met with cold, emotionally-unavailable parents, their development becomes compromised.

When a child feels as though they are not being seen by their parents, their emotional needs will not be met, therefore their mental and emotional world becomes underdeveloped.

This style of parenting is heavily tied to the lack of empathy that a narcissist displays.

The 'coldness' that a child feels from a neglectful parent is very confusing for them, often this feeling pushes the child into developing a people-pleaser mentality to get noticed and validated.

The disconnect that the parent has created doesn't allow the child to build healthy, loving connected relationships, they will have difficulty forming secure attachments with others, chances are they will develop unhealthy attachments to feel wanted. This neglectful style of parenting can lead to problems with trust and intimacy in adulthood.

It is not uncommon for a child who does not feel loved and wanted to start to seek validation elsewhere. This can be very dangerous for a child as they may engage in risky behaviours in order to gain attention from others. These behaviours can include substance abuse, self-harm and risky sexual behaviour.

- **Being excessively criticised for their behaviours**
  – Damaging self-esteem

Excessive criticism teaches children that they are not good enough and they are not capable of achieving their goals, it can also make them feel inadequate, flawed, worthless and will discourage them from trying new things. It can also make a child feel like they are not worthy of love and acceptance, excessive criticism develops a belief that they are only valuable if they are perfect. This can lead to a lifelong pattern of self-criticism and self-doubt, making it difficult for them to reach their full potential.

Excessive criticism can also teach children how to project their anger, which becomes a coping mechanism to deflect feelings of regret and embarrassment. This coping mechanism becomes a protective barrier that eventually blocks all forms of criticism. It develops a 'victim' mindset where the child learns to focus on how unfairly others treat them rather than what's needed to improve themselves, thus not developing a sense of accountability for their actions.

Induced shame is harmful for children as it develops a belief they are flawed and unable to change. This is where narcissistic rage develops into adulthood as a coping strategy to feel safe. They may use this rage to assert their dominance, to intimidate others or to manipulate others in order to feel powerful and in control.

- **Overvaluing the child**
  – Teaching them their status in society

It isn't a bad thing to love and cherish your child. This is healthy. In the eyes of many parents, they believe their child is the most beautiful they have ever seen, which is wonderful and is a sign of unconditional love. This belief, however, becomes a problem when parents teach their child early on that they are superior to everyone else and deserve special treatment because of their perceived 'value'.

Parents who are invested in their child's success and constantly push them to excel in order to show off the child's value, places unrealistic expectations on them. This pressure to perform and meet the parents' expectations, can lead to feelings of inadequacy and low self-esteem.

Parents who overvalue their child, will not accept any flaws and will push to make their child believe that they are 'better' than everyone else. This pushing has the ability to develop into an inflated sense of self and the child becoming entitled. The child then learns that they should receive a high level of attention and admiration for their status in society which is very damaging when it comes to building relationships.

When a child is given an excessive amount of unjustified praise, this sets up a superiority belief that gets carried through into adult life, with a desired need for attention in order for that person's needs to be met. This style of parenting doesn't allow a child to learn how to set realistic goals for themselves. They will struggle to handle setbacks and may be overwhelmed when they are faced with the reality that they are not as talented or special as they have been led to believe.

- **Narcissistic parent(s)**
  – Controlling, unpredictable parenting style

Narcissists need to control every aspect of their child's life. They need to appear as the 'perfect parent'. This is because they see their child as an extension of themselves, so when their child is doing well in life, whether that be in sports or academically, they will be the child's biggest cheerleader. They will be seen to be pushing their child and doing everything in their power to make that child succeed. They will appear to the outside world as a fantastic parent and the reason for their child's success, but this success is a double-edged sword for a narcissist. They will be filled with jealousy if they have a talented, popular child. When a narcissistic parent is jealous of their child they may try to compete with their child, in an attempt to prove that they are more capable or talented. There will be moments when the parent will take the spotlight away from their child, wanting all the attention on them as the loving, supportive parent who enabled the child to become such a success.

Many narcissistic parents also resent their child for having the energy and opportunities that they no longer have, as a result they become overly possessive of their child and do not allow the child to develop their own identity. If, however, they have a child who is perhaps shy and not extremely talented, they will belittle that child and reinforce how much of a failure that child is, sometimes even reinforcing to the child what an embarrassment they are to the family. This belittling is done specifically to tear down their child's confidence and make themselves feel superior. This kind of belittling causes the child to feel ashamed of themselves and their actions. Narcissistic parents often compare the child to others, leading the child to feel inadequate and embarrassed. Narcissists are manipulative, and will use manipulation to control and make the child feel guilty or embarrassed for not meeting their expectations.

The treatment children receive behind closed doors by a narcissistic parent creates an anxious child with very low self-esteem. There is an immense amount of mental and emotional abuse that a child will suffer when they are raised by a narcissistic parent.

The intense highs and lows that a child experiences in their upbringing develops into either a people-pleasing lifestyle or they will develop that narcissistic shell and become mirror images of their parent(s).

Triangulation is a manipulation technique often used by narcissistic parents to control and maintain power over their children. It involves creating a third party or situation that serves to pit one child against another, or to create alliances that serve the narcissistic parent's agenda.

Narcissistic parents and triangulation

Triangulation is a much-loved technique that a narcissist will typically use to create conflict or competition between siblings. This can be done in a number of ways, such as:

- **Favouritism:** The narcissistic parent may show favouritism towards one child over the other, showering them with attention, gifts and praise, while neglecting or criticising the other child. This creates jealousy and resentment between the siblings, and can also lead to the 'unfavoured' child showing the narcissist more attention in a bid to become the favoured child.

- **Scapegoating:** The narcissistic parent may scapegoat one child, blaming them for everything that goes wrong in the family and treating them with hostility and criticism. This creates a sense of isolation and alienation for the targeted child.

Children who are used as a scapegoat will experience feelings of shame, inadequacy and a sense of being unlovable. They will then believe that they are never good enough, and that their efforts are never recognised or appreciated.

- **Comparison:** The narcissistic parent may constantly compare the siblings, highlighting the achievements and successes of one, while downplaying or dismissing those of the other. This creates a sense of competition and insecurity between the siblings. The child who is constantly compared to their sibling may feel inadequate and develop feelings of inferiority, while the favoured child may develop a sense of entitlement, which can lead to narcissistic tendencies later in life.

- **Secrets:** The narcissistic parent may share secrets or confidences with one child, creating a sense of exclusivity and bonding between them, while excluding the other child. This creates a sense of betrayal and mistrust for the targeted child. Children who experience this kind of isolation will struggle to trust others, and as a result will impact their ability to form healthy relationships later in life.

All of these styles of parenting create long-term mental and emotional health issues.

Many children who are raised in one of these environments will experience anxiety and depression, as they will feel neglected and unimportant.

Raising a child is by no means easy and no parent is perfect, most are trying to do their best in a world that is full of pressures and expectations. I often get asked if it's possible to prevent narcissism from being cultivated. While there is no conclusive answer to how it is created, parenting styles do impact a child's mental and emotional development.

In order for certain parenting styles to transition into a healthier style it would require the parents to become aware of how they are choosing to raise their child, and change any toxic parenting behaviours that are not supporting their child's growth. This can involve setting boundaries, being consistent with discipline and encouraging children to take on age-appropriate responsibilities.

It is important for parents to provide guidance and structure while also allowing children to make their own decisions and take responsibility for their actions in order to promote healthy mental and emotional growth.

Parenting has a significant influence on a child's development, shaping their personality, behaviour and self-esteem. Therefore, parents need to provide their children with a healthy environment that fosters emotional intelligence, empathy and a sense of community.

Can a child be diagnosed as a 'narcissist' early on and can it be prevented?

No, a child cannot be diagnosed with Narcissistic Personality Disorder (NPD); it requires an individual to be at least eighteen years old before they can receive a diagnosis because personality traits and patterns are considered to be relatively stable and consistent over time. It takes time for a person's personality to fully develop and become relatively stable. Therefore, it is important to observe the individual's behaviour, thoughts and emotions over a prolonged period before making a diagnosis of NPD.

Furthermore, many of the symptoms of NPD, such as a grandiose sense of self-importance, a lack of empathy and an excessive need for admiration, are often present in typical teenage behaviour. These symptoms may be a part of normal adolescent development, and it can be difficult to distinguish between normal behaviour and the presence of a personality disorder.

Finally, it is important to note that diagnosing a personality disorder in a child or adolescent can be challenging because their personalities are still developing and changing. It is essential to avoid labelling a child or adolescent with a personality disorder prematurely, as this can be harmful to their self-esteem and can limit their potential for growth and change.

If you believe that your child is exhibiting narcissistic tendencies, it is important to seek the advice of a mental health professional who specialises in child and adolescent psychology. A mental health professional can help you determine if your child's behaviour is indicative of a personality disorder or if it is just a part of normal adolescent development. They can also provide you with strategies for managing your child's behaviour and help you develop a plan for addressing any underlying issues that may be contributing to their behaviour.

If you do decide to take your child to see a mental health professional it is important you don't create a stigma around the process. Therapy is very valuable when you are looking to develop your mental and emotional health, it is not something that someone undertakes just because they are 'sick'.

Here are several things that you can do as a parent to help your child manage their behaviour and develop healthy habits and relationships:

- **Set clear boundaries and consequences for inappropriate behaviour.** Make sure your child understands what is expected of them and the consequences of their actions. Boundaries don't work unless they have consequences tied to them which you are prepared to follow through on.

- **Encourage empathy and emotional intelligence.** Help your child develop the ability to understand and identify their own emotions as well as the emotions of others.

- **Model healthy behaviour.** Show your child what healthy relationships and behaviour look like by modelling appropriate behaviour yourself. This will require you to address any unhealthy behaviours that you are currently displaying.

- **Provide unconditional love and support.** Make sure your child knows they are loved and supported, regardless of their behaviour.

- **Encourage your child to seek professional help.** If your child is exhibiting narcissistic tendencies, it may be beneficial for them to seek professional help to address any underlying issues and develop healthy habits and relationships. Let your child know that therapy is good, and is something that many turn to when they need help.

Remember that parenting a child with narcissistic tendencies can be challenging, but with the right support and strategies, it is possible to help your child develop into a healthy and happy adult.

Narcissistic cultures

There are several cultures where narcissistic behaviour may be viewed as a sign of strength or success rather than a negative trait. These cultures tend to place a high value on individual achievement, assertiveness and self-promotion.

Some examples include:

• **Western cultures:** Many Western societies, particularly those in North America and Europe, place a high value on individualism and self-promotion. In these cultures, being assertive and confident is often seen as a key to success, and those who are able to promote themselves effectively are often admired and rewarded.

• **Asian cultures:** In some Asian cultures, such as China and Japan, there is a strong emphasis on competition and success. In these cultures, individuals who are able to achieve a high level of success and status are often admired, even if they exhibit narcissistic behaviour.

• **Middle-eastern cultures:** In some Middle Eastern cultures, particularly those that place a high value on wealth and power, narcissistic behaviour may be seen as a sign of strength and success. In these cultures, individuals who are able to accumulate wealth and exert influence over others, may be viewed as powerful and successful.

It's important to note that while some cultures may view narcissistic behaviour as a positive trait, this is not universally true. In many cultures, narcissistic behaviour is still viewed as negative and may be met with disapproval or criticism. Additionally, even in cultures where narcissistic behaviour is viewed positively, there may be limits to what is considered acceptable behaviour.

Genetic and neurological factors that may contribute to the development of narcissism

There have been several studies conducted on the genetic and neurological factors that may contribute to the development of narcissism.

Here are a few examples:

- **Genetic factors:** In a study published in the *Journal of Personality* in 2011, researchers examined the role of genetics in narcissism by looking at the personality traits of 130 pairs of identical twins and 147 pairs of fraternal twins. The study found that identical twins, who share 100% of their genes, were more similar in their levels of narcissism than fraternal twins, who share only 50% of their genes. This suggests that genetics may play a role in the development of narcissism.

- **Brain imaging:** In a study published in the *Journal Social Cognitive and Affective Neuroscience* in 2016, researchers used fMRI brain imaging to examine the neural correlates of narcissism. The study found that individuals with higher levels of narcissism showed greater activation in brain regions associated with reward processing when they received positive feedback about themselves. This suggests that narcissists may have a heightened sensitivity to rewards and positive feedback, which may contribute to their inflated sense of self-importance.

- **Neurological impairments:** In a study published in the journal *Personality Disorders* in 2015, researchers examined the relationship between narcissism and impairments in executive functioning, which refers to a set of cognitive processes involved in goal-directed behaviour. The study found that individuals with higher levels of narcissism showed impairments in their ability to plan, organise and execute complex tasks. This suggests that narcissists may have deficits in their executive functioning that contribute to their grandiosity and lack of empathy.

- **Epigenetic factors:** In a study published in the journal *Frontiers in Psychology* in 2019, researchers examined the role of epigenetic factors in the development of narcissism. Epigenetic factors refer to changes in gene expression that are not caused by alterations to the underlying DNA sequence. The study found that individuals with higher levels of narcissism showed epigenetic changes in genes associated with stress response, which may contribute to their hypersensitivity to criticism and their tendency to lash out when their self-esteem is threatened.

These are just a few examples of the research that has been conducted on the genetic and neurological factors that may contribute to the development of narcissism. While these studies provide valuable insights into the underlying mechanisms of narcissism, it is important to note that the causes of this personality disorder are complex and multifaceted, and it is likely that they involve a combination of genetic, environmental and social factors.

2
Social Media and Narcissism

Has social media contributed to the development of narcissism?

In today's digital age, social media has become a ubiquitous part of our lives. We use it to connect with friends and family, share our experiences and express our opinions. While social media has many benefits, it has also been linked to the development of narcissism.

The characterised traits of narcissists seem to fit well with how social media platforms function. In recent years, researchers have started to investigate the relationship between social media use and narcissism, and the results have been revealing.

One study published in *Journal of Personality and Social Psychology* found that social media use was positively associated with narcissistic traits such as exhibitionism, entitlement and self-absorption. The study, which surveyed over 1,600 adults, found that those who used social media frequently tended to have higher levels of narcissism.

Another study published in the journal *Personality and Individual Differences* found that individuals who used social media frequently tended to have lower levels of empathy, which is another key component of narcissism. The study surveyed over 300 adults and found that those who used social media more often were less likely to feel empathy towards others.

So why does social media contribute to the development of narcissism?

There are several factors at play. Firstly, social media provides a platform for self-promotion and validation. People can post pictures and updates about their lives, and receive likes and comments from their followers. This constant feedback can create a sense of self-importance and entitlement, as individuals begin to believe that their lives are more interesting and important than others.

Secondly, social media creates a culture of comparison. People are constantly exposed to the highlight reels of others' lives, which can create feelings of envy and inadequacy. In an effort to keep up with the Joneses, individuals may engage in more self-promotion and seek even more validation from others.

Finally, social media can lead to a decrease in face-to-face interaction and a lack of genuine connection. Instead of building real relationships, individuals may prioritise their online persona and the validation it brings. This can lead to a lack of empathy and a focus on self-promotion, further reinforcing narcissistic tendencies.

So what can we do to counteract the negative effects of social media on our sense of self-worth and well-being? Here are a few tips:

- **Practise mindfulness.** Take a break from social media and focus on the present moment. Engage in activities that bring you joy and fulfilment, without seeking validation from others via an online platform.

- **Build genuine relationships.** Spend time with loved ones and engage in face-to-face interactions. Cultivate empathy and connection by actively listening and engaging with others.

- **Be aware of your social media use.** Set boundaries and limit your time on social media. Be mindful of what content you are consuming and how you feel after scrolling through your feed. Don't be afraid to remove anyone from your feed who doesn't leave you feeling good.

- **Practise self-compassion**. Remember that everyone has flaws and imperfections. Be kind and gentle with yourself, and avoid comparing yourself to others. If you recognise yourself doing this then it is time to take a complete break and focus on yourself.

I am not saying that social media is bad, because it does also have many benefits. When you are mindful of how you use social media, you can build genuine relationships and you can use it to further educate yourself and to practise self-compassion. It is all about learning to counteract the negative effects that social media can have on you and cultivate a healthy sense of self-worth and well-being.

The impact of social media documentation on a child's mental and emotional health

'You cannot raise your children the way your parents raised you. Because your parents were raised in a world where social media didn't exist.'

Children who have grown up in the digital age, have likely experienced their parents documenting their child's life through social media. From posting photos of their first steps to sharing their academic achievements, social media has become a way for parents to celebrate their child's milestones and share their joy with family and friends. While this may seem harmless, constant documentation can have negative effects on a child's mental and emotional health. Childhood is a time for learning and growth. When a child grows up in a world where their every move is documented and shared online, it can have a profound impact on their mental and emotional health.

Here are a few ways in which constant social media documentation can impact a child:

- **It can create a feeling of pressure:** When a child's every milestone is documented and shared online, it can create a sense of pressure to constantly perform and achieve. This pressure can be overwhelming for a child and can lead to feelings of anxiety and stress.

- **It can impact their sense of privacy:** Children have a right to privacy, and constant social media documentation can infringe on that right. As they grow older, they may feel uncomfortable with the level of personal information that has been shared about them online, leading to feelings of vulnerability and insecurity.

- **It can impact their self-esteem:** When a child's life is constantly documented and shared online, it can impact their self-esteem. They may feel like they have to look and act a certain way to be accepted, leading to feelings of inadequacy and low self-esteem.

- **It can impact their relationships:** As a child grows up, they may feel embarrassed or uncomfortable with the level of personal information that has been shared about them online. This can impact their relationships with peers and family members, as they may feel like their privacy has been violated.

- **It can create a distorted view of reality:** Social media is often a highlight reel of people's lives, and constant documentation can create a distorted view of reality for a child. They may feel like their life is not measuring up to the curated images and stories that are being shared online, leading to feelings of inadequacy and self-doubt.

Parents who are narcissistic will be doing this purely for their own benefit to get attention and validation for what an amazing parent they are. It is important for parents to ask themselves why they feel it is necessary to constantly be taking pictures and videos of their children to post online. Remember that everything that your child initially learns about social media, in terms of how it works and what it is used for, is from their parents.

What can parents do?

As a parent, it's important to be mindful of the impact that constant social media documentation can have on your child's mental and emotional health. Here are a few tips to help minimise the negative effects:

- **Set boundaries:** It's important to set boundaries around what you share online about your child. Consider asking your child's permission before posting photos or updates about them. And if your child declines to be videoed or photographed don't force them to do it, instead respect their decision.

- **Respect your child's privacy**: As your child grows older, be mindful of the level of personal information that you share online about them. Respect their privacy and ask for their consent before sharing personal details.

- **Prioritise quality time:** Instead of constantly documenting your child's life, prioritise quality time together. Spend time doing activities that you both enjoy, without the pressure of having to document every moment.

- **Encourage self-expression:** Encourage your child to express themselves in ways that don't involve social media. This can include creative activities like drawing or painting, or physical activities like sports and exercise.

- **Practise mindfulness:** It's important to be mindful of the impact that social media is having on your child's mental and emotional health. Take time to reflect on your social media use and how it's impacting your child, and make adjustments as needed.

In conclusion, constant social media documentation can have a profound impact on a child's mental and emotional health. As a parent, it's important to be mindful of the impact that social media is having on your child and to take steps to minimise the negative effects it can have.

Here are some studies that were conducted on the impact of social media documentation on a child's mental and emotional health.

1. A study published in the journal *Cyberpsychology, Behavior, and Social Networking* found that parents who frequently post about their children on social media may be unintentionally harming their child's sense of privacy. The study surveyed over 700 parents and found that parents who frequently posted about their children on social media had children who were more likely to feel like their privacy had been violated (Fardouly, Diedrichs, Vartanian, & Halliwell, 2015).

2. Another study published in the journal *Computers in Human Behavior* found that children who are frequently photographed for social media may experience negative psychological outcomes, such as anxiety and stress. The study surveyed over 200 parents and found that children who were photographed more frequently for social media experienced more anxiety and stress than children who were photographed less frequently (Boyd & Ellison, 2007).

3. A study published in the journal *Pediatrics* found that parents who frequently posted about their children on social media may be unintentionally exposing their children to online risks, such as cyberbullying and identity theft. The study surveyed over 2,000 parents and found that parents who frequently posted about their children on social media were less likely to be aware of online risks and less likely to take steps to protect their children online (Moreno, Egan, Barek, & Ganahl, 2015).

3

Am I a Narcissist?

This question comes up a lot. With more people talking about their narcissistic exes and bosses, narcissism is becoming a buzzword that most of us don't fully understand. We tend to think that someone who is selfish is a narcissist, or someone who prides themselves on their appearance and loves to take selfies, is one too. While these behaviours can constitute displaying narcissistic traits, it takes more than just one or two of these traits to amount to a personality disorder. Finding yourself asking if you are a narcissist, is a good sign! If you then recognise certain toxic traits and behaviours that you're displaying and you are willing to put in the effort to change them, then the answer is likely no, you're not a narcissist.

Long story short, narcissism is an extreme self-involvement that makes a person ignore the needs of those around them and always put themselves first. I do want to make it clear that we can all occasionally display narcissistic behaviour, but true narcissists with a personality disorder will frequently disregard others or their feelings to the point where it can be deeply wounding for those around them. Due to their inability to empathise, true narcissists also do not understand the effect that their behaviour has on other individuals, as people with a narcissistic personality disorder do not feel empathy.

Empathy on the other hand is the complete opposite to narcissism.

Those who have empathy are often described as sensitive. This is because those with empathy have an ability to understand what other people feel, and see things from their point of view on an emotional level. Those who have a high level of empathy are in touch with their emotions and can 'feel' what the other person is feeling, tuning into that person's pain or happiness as if it was their own. Having a good level of empathy is what allows us to connect and build successful relationships. Empathy, like narcissism, can be developed, and it is one of the key elements of emotional intelligence.

Emotional empathy allows individuals to feel a sense of shared emotional experience with others, which can create feelings of closeness, intimacy and mutual understanding. It can also help individuals to provide emotional support and comfort to others during times of need, as they are able to fully connect with, and understand, the other person's emotional experience. For example, if a friend is going through a difficult breakup and is feeling sad and upset, emotional empathy allows you to truly understand and share in their emotional experience. This can help you to provide comfort and support that is more genuine and meaningful than if you were simply sympathising or offering advice without fully connecting with their emotions.

However emotional empathy can also be challenging at times, as it can involve experiencing negative emotions alongside others. This can be difficult to manage, especially if the emotions are intense or overwhelming. It is important to practise self-care and emotional-regulation strategies in order to manage these emotions and maintain healthy emotional boundaries.

People often get confused and believe that narcissists can feel empathy. But this is a different type of *empathy* and one that can be learned. A narcissist can show an understanding of how to connect with others using a learnt skill called cognitive empathy. Unlike emotional empathy, which involves sharing in another person's emotional experience and feeling their emotions as if they were your own, cognitive empathy allows individuals to understand and relate to another person's emotional experience without necessarily experiencing the same emotions themselves.

Those who practise cognitive empathy have an ability to understand and interpret another person's thoughts, emotions and perspectives, without necessarily sharing the same emotional experience as the other person. This is how a narcissist appears to be 'in tune' with their victims. They seem to be able to recognise and appreciate another person's feelings, as well as being able to accurately identify and respond to their needs and desires.

Cognitive empathy is an important skill for effective communication and building positive relationships with others. When someone is able to do this, it means that you can show that you understand the other person's perspective. When a narcissist masters this skill, they will give the impression that they can truly care about you and as a result can connect with you on a deeper level.

Narcissists put this skill into action by asking intense questions about you and your life, without much desire to share any of theirs with you. This is extremely common on a first date. The idea that they know 'everything' about you makes you feel like there's a connection. The narcissist will display a deep level of understanding around how you feel and the experiences that have shaped you, but they won't genuinely be able to connect. Here is an example: you are told by your friend that their mother has been diagnosed with terminal cancer and your friend is deeply upset.

As someone who has empathy, they will likely respond in a way that shows an expression of sadness, saying something along the lines of "I'm so sorry to hear about your mother. I know this must be so hard for both of you. I'm here for you if you need anything please don't hesitate to ask" – showing a sincerity to help and if you do reach out to help that person will be available and willing to help.

For someone who practises cognitive empathy they are likely to respond with little visible emotion and will understand what needs to be said by responding with something like "I'm sorry. I know you are sad and that what you are going through is hard" – highly unlikely to include an offer to help and if you do ask for help it will be difficult for them to be able to assist you. They are likely to come up with an excuse of why they can't help. The words used are not always an obvious give away, it is the lack of visible emotion or the amount of emotion shown which indicates the type of empathy being displayed.

When we function off intense emotions it is difficult to think clearly and logically as we are overwhelmed by the emotion. This is often the reason cognitive empathy gets missed, and you didn't see that person's true nature.

Narcissism is considered a spectrum disorder because it encompasses a wide range of behaviours and traits that can manifest in different ways and to different degrees. The severity of narcissistic traits can vary greatly from person to person, ranging from a few narcissistic traits to the full-blown personality disorder with very fixed toxic traits. The clinical name for the personality disorder is NPD – Narcissistic Personality Disorder.

Those who are at the top end of the spectrum and have the personality disorder, cannot be cured. Personality disorders are life-long conditions that can potentially be treated, but those with this disorder will tend to avoid psychotherapy or will often quit prematurely when they feel threatened or uncomfortable.

Starting the processes requires them to face their own underlying shame and low self-esteem. This is a problem for someone who has this type of disorder. The narcissistic shell that was created keeps them 'safe' believing that nothing is wrong with them, so getting treatment would be a waste of time and money. Also, their superiority makes it incredibly difficult for a therapist to work with them.

Those with this disorder do not think that anyone could possibly know more than them. Therefore, a therapist could not help them. This attitude also makes them want to 'test' the therapist rather than work with them. This can result in them staying in therapy for years without any real results. More often than not the only time you will find a narcissist in therapy is when they have been ordered to by the courts!

Often an addiction of sorts tends to accompany someone with this personality disorder.

Addictions can be treated, again, if the individual wants to deal with the addiction, it can be done. This is also the same for any mental health issues that arise such as depression or anxiety, both of these can be successfully treated with medication and psychotherapy. It is usually mental health issues and addictions that will push someone with NPD into getting some help, but often it won't be for their toxic behaviours.

The narcissistic spectrum

At the entry level of the spectrum, we have 'healthy' narcissism, and at the top end, we have 'pathological' which is where we find the personality disorder.

Healthy narcissism

It should come as no surprise that healthy narcissism is typically developed during childhood through positive experiences of being seen and valued by caregivers and others in the child's environment. When caregivers provide a warm, nurturing and responsive environment, children learn that they are valued and loved for who they are, and they develop a positive sense of self-worth.

As children grow and develop, they begin to explore and assert their own needs and desires while also learning to navigate the needs and desires of others. Through this process, they develop a healthy balance between self-focus and other-focus, which allows them to form positive relationships with others and to pursue their own goals and interests.

Healthy narcissism is an important component of psychological well-being, as it allows individuals to develop a positive sense of self-worth and to pursue their goals and interests, while also forming positive relationships with others.

People who have a healthy level of narcissism, display flexible, adaptive traits such as confidence and a high level of self-awareness with a positive sense of self, where the individual understands their value and their limitations. Those with a healthy level of narcissism don't perceive their strengths and weaknesses as something that defines who they are. They will be open to criticism, and often seek advice from others to learn more about themselves in order to grow and progress. They will have no problem working with others, understanding that teamwork can get you to an end goal quickly. Many would describe this person as someone who is strong and humble. The healthy level of narcissism shows up as a desire for attention and admiration, but this desire does not interfere with an individual's ability to form healthy relationships or function in daily life.

Level 2

I would describe this level as a transition phase. This is where you would find a 'normal' level of narcissism which is often triggered when there is a shift in someone's lifestyle, for instance a person's job role. They get promoted to a more senior role and their behaviour completely changes – and not necessarily in a good way.

The truth is many roles of power require someone to have a level of narcissism in order for them to be successful. These people tend to be leaders, and would have sufficient responsibilities that require a certain set of skills to get the best outcomes, hence where the transition comes into play.

The question here then becomes: *do you stay humble?* Or, do you take on a belief that you got the promotion *because you are better than everyone else and those around you need to understand this and automatically show you respect.*

This level of narcissism is semi-flexible, meaning it can switch between a healthy to a more dangerous toxic level. It can be difficult for someone to find a balance, but that doesn't mean it's impossible. Having a good amount of confidence in your abilities to get the job done places you in the 'healthy' level of narcissism category. This crosses over into the toxic level if this confidence is accompanied with arrogance, a feeling of superiority over others and an expectation of being treated as 'special' due to your job role. The way to avoid this toxic switch is by having a high level of self-awareness, and also being open to taking feedback from others about your behaviour.

New-found wealth also has a role to play when you look at level 2 narcissism. Those who cross over into the toxic side believe that with wealth comes power and a degree of respect. The undercurrent of this belief holds a sense of entitlement which is a core component of NPD. The saying 'money changes people' holds a lot of truth when you are dealing with someone who has narcissistic traits and is in the process of switching through level 2.

The good news is, if you do find yourself at this level, switching in and out of displaying toxic traits, then you have a high chance of successfully removing them should you seek help.

Level 3

This is where 'toxic' narcissistic traits start to become more dominant and that person's inner emotional world becomes more vacant and numb. Empathy stops being practised, it becomes non-existent and validation becomes the game and requirement for someone who is moving through to this level of narcissism, as this is what they need to thrive.

This validation will be sought from the outside world on a very frequent basis, using various techniques to ensure they get it. Attention seeking is a great way to validate their self-worth. Using various tools to grab attention, such as talking loudly, interrupting others or telling grandiose stories which they LOVE to do on social media.

Social media platforms really are a narcissist playground as it's by far the easiest and quickest way to get validation by posting provocative or boastful updates to gain likes and comments.

A great indicator that someone is on this level is by how they seek validation and what they do with it. Everything that a toxic narcissist does is for a purpose and it's a selfish purpose. They will expect life to revolve around them without a care in the world for anyone else. And should anyone question them about their behaviour they will either become very defensive or claim to be a victim as a result of being caught out.

Selfies are an interesting topic with many believing that selfie takers are all narcissists. While there is an element of truth to this, the reality is that anyone can take a selfie and it's become very acceptable in today's society. But, it all depends on their motive and what outcome the person who took the selfie is looking to achieve, and the pattern in which they take and post them. Someone who is at this level or above will post selfies with the focus being on how many likes, comments and shares they can get. This will become an obsession for them, and will become part of their identity, frequently commenting about how 'popular' they are.

All of these interactions will feed their ego and temporarily satisfy their need for validation. They will post daily, often more than once with a consistent pattern of selfies and what would be defined as 'clickbait' images that have no real content behind them.

There is also a good possibility that the selfie will be provocative or showing an item of high value. For them, this is important as it connects to their belief of being special and having a sought-after status due to the material objects they possess.

This is also often done in an attempt to make others envious. A clear sign the selfie taker is high in narcissism, is that the picture will be very superficial. Likewise, if you weren't a frequent selfie taker and you had purchased a new handbag that you were very proud of, and you wanted to take a picture of yourself with the bag to mark the occasion, then this would not make you a narcissist.

What is clickbait?

Clickbait images are tools that a business may use to attract clicks and generate traffic to websites or social media pages. The images that are used often have little to do with the content of the article or post and are designed solely to grab the viewer's attention.

Narcissists tend to use clickbait images for validation in a few different ways:

- Narcissists crave attention and admiration, and using provocative images can be a way for them to get the attention they crave, thus giving them the attention and validation they need.

- Narcissists often have an inflated sense of self-importance and may believe that they are so attractive or desirable that they can use clickbait images to manipulate others. This is done to fuel their own sense of grandiosity.

- Narcissists also use these images to control others. Clickbait images are a way to lure people into their false reality, as a result they can manipulate them into doing what they want.

Other than validation, a narcissist will also use clickbait images as a tool for manipulation and as a way to gain further control over their partner. Here are some examples:

- The narcissist will post a picture of themselves with a member of their sexual preference or will engage in flirty behaviour online which is done in an obvious manner, with the intention to make their partner jealous or to create a sense of competition.

• The narcissist will also use clickbait images to blackmail their partner. For example, they may take a compromising picture of their partner and threaten to share it publicly if they don't comply with their demands.

• The narcissist may use clickbait images to manipulate their partner into feeling guilty. For example, they may post a picture of themselves looking sad or distressed and imply that their partner is to blame. This can create a sense of obligation or guilt that the partner feels they need to rectify. Should the partner react, this would confirm to the narcissist that they have a high level of control over that partner.

Level 4

This is the top end of the spectrum, the pathological/clinical end. This is where you will find cluster B personality disorders which are characterised by very rigid toxic traits.

• **Narcissistic Personality Disorder (NPD)** – This is a personality disorder characterised by a grandiose sense of self-importance, a lack of empathy for others and a need for admiration. People with NPD often have an inflated sense of their own abilities and achievements and may become envious of others who they perceive as being more successful.

• **Antisocial Personality Disorder (ASPD)** – This is a personality disorder characterised by a disregard for the rights of others and a lack of empathy. People with ASPD often engage in impulsive and irresponsible behaviour, violate the law and exploit others for personal gain.

• **Borderline Personality Disorder (BPD)** – While not strictly a "narcissistic" disorder, BPD often involves a deep sense of emptiness, instability in interpersonal relationships and an intense fear of abandonment. People with BPD may engage in impulsive and self-destructive behaviour and can have difficulty regulating their emotions.

- **Histrionic Personality Disorder (HPD)** – This is a personality disorder characterised by excessive emotionality and attention-seeking behaviour. People with HPD may crave attention and validation from others and may use their appearance, behaviour or emotions to elicit a response from others.

Sadism is also a personality trait that some in this category will practise.

Many may think of sadism in a sexual or criminal context, sadistic tendencies are however common in everyday life and there is a link between sadism and those who are at the pathological end of the narcissistic spectrum.

An everyday sadist is someone who derives pleasure or satisfaction from causing harm or pain to others in everyday situations, such as through teasing, criticising or humiliating them. Sadists enjoy seeing others suffer and may go out of their way to create situations where they can exert power and control over others. This behaviour often ties into narcissism because both traits involve a lack of empathy and a desire for dominance over others. Narcissists may engage in everyday sadism as a way to assert their superiority and maintain their sense of control over others. They may also use it as a means of deflecting attention away from their own insecurities and flaws by focussing on the faults and weaknesses of others.

It's important to note that not all everyday sadists are necessarily narcissistic, and not all narcissists engage in everyday sadism. However, the two traits are closely linked, and individuals who exhibit one trait may be more likely to exhibit the other as well. Understanding the connection between everyday sadism and narcissism is helpful in identifying and addressing these harmful behaviours in oneself or others.

As narcissism develops, that person's need to feel wanted and validated at all times becomes a way of life for them. So, whenever a narcissist feels rejected or they are disappointed in your behaviour, their frail egos get hurt, and they will react negatively in ways which ultimately give them back their power. It's this power and control that allows a narcissist to feel 'safe'. As humans, instinctively we are always looking for safety in our environment.

Some of the common power play responses include:

- **Anger/narcissistic rage** – Tantrums, physical attacks, throwing objects to intimidate.

- **Passive aggression** – Giving you the cold shoulder, the silent treatment, withholding love and affection, being sarcastic and rude, threatening separation.

- **Emotional coercion** – Blaming you, guilt-tripping you, calling their partner ungrateful, pretend victimhood.

All of these responses are learnt behaviours that a narcissist has developed in order for them to feel safe and in control. More often than not all three of these powerplay responses are commonly used when you are dealing with someone who is at this level.

Understand that when it comes to being in a relationship with a narcissist, they are incapable of building and nurturing emotional bonds with others.

When you find yourself being in such a dysfunctional relationship, you will likely find yourself doing most of the heavy emotional lifting – this is a clear sign that you are NOT a narcissist and should also run away!

I want you to understand that everyone may exhibit some narcissistic traits from time to time, but that does not necessarily mean that you are a full-blown narcissist. In fact, it is a good sign and a strong indication that you are not a narcissist if you find yourself concerned about your behaviour or the impact it is having on others, and you are wanting to put in the effort to make changes.

In the next chapter we will go deep into everything that constitutes NPD.

4

How to Spot a Narcissist

A narcissist looks no different to any other human. Big egos come in all shapes, sizes, genders and ages. All are unique and although many often lead 'normal' lives it has been proven that certain types of narcissists thrive in certain roles. This can make them easier to spot.

There is a belief that there are more narcissistic men than women, however, there is no conclusive evidence to suggest that narcissism is more prevalent in one gender than the other. I do believe, however, that there are some slight differences between the two in the specific traits that they display. Men, from my experience, are more likely to display exhibitionism and superiority, while women are more likely to display a need for attention and admiration.

NPD is a clinical diagnosis that is recognised in the fifth edition of the *Diagnostic and Statistical Manual of Mental Health Disorders (DSM-5).* An individual needs the presence of at least five out of the following nine listed below to meet the criteria:

1. A grandiose sense of self-importance
2. A preoccupation with fantasies of unlimited power, success, brilliance or beauty
3. A belief that he/she is special and unique and can only be understood by, or should associate with, other special or high-status people
4. A need for excessive admiration
5. A sense of entitlement
6. Interpersonally exploitative behaviour
7. A lack of empathy

8. Envy of others or a belief that others are envious of them
9. A demonstration of arrogant and haughty behaviours or attitudes

For someone to get this diagnosis they need to show a consistent pattern of behaviour, with regular occurrences of the traits above. But, getting this diagnosis isn't as easy as it would seem, as not all narcissists behave the same. And something that a narcissist does very well is lie!

NPD is the one of the least-diagnosed disorders as many narcissists lie to avoid getting what they would perceive to be 'exposed', exposed for who they truly are beneath the mask and grandiose bravado they display. Understand that for them, the way they live their life, kind of works, so, why would they need to change? This is what makes getting a diagnosis and treatment for them very difficult.

A narcissist's manipulation tactics allow them to have a life that grants them power and admiration which is what they seek. More often than not, when they manage to snare a victim, that victim will remain in their lives for a very long time as their 'supply' to use and abuse when it suits them.

When many hear the term 'narcissistic supply' they immediately think 'lovers'. Yes, narcissists' lovers are indeed a form of supply for them but narcissists can also find their supply in many different ways.

A narcissist needs these three things:

1. **Attention**
2. **Admiration**
3. **Validation**

When these core needs are met, a narcissist's self-importance and grandiosity will be maintained. Narcissists need this supply to feel good about themselves and to boost their self-esteem.

The way that a narcissist gets their supply is via compliments, praise, adoration, attention, and even fear or intimidation. The key factor is that it must be focussed on the narcissist and reinforce their sense of superiority and specialness. Narcissists will go to great lengths to obtain this supply, often manipulating others or engaging in attention-seeking behaviours to get the attention and validation they need. This is where multiple lovers come in. Narcissists will use a variety of tactics to obtain and maintain their 'lovers' supply. Acting charming and charismatic, they are using their charisma to attract others and gain their admiration. They will also be manipulative, using guilt, shame or fear to control their lovers and keep them under their influence. In extreme cases with those who are at the top end of the spectrum, they may resort to threats or violence to maintain their sense of power and control.

What is narcissistic supply?

The use of narcissistic supply is not limited to personal relationships. In professional settings, narcissists may seek out positions of power or authority in order to gain the attention and admiration of others. They may also engage in attention-seeking behaviours, such as self-promotion or taking credit for the work of others, in order to maintain their sense of importance and superiority.

The need for narcissistic supply is a defining characteristic of those with a high degree of narcissism. It is a key part of the narcissist's self-identity, and they will go to great lengths to obtain it, always at the expense of others. Understanding this need for supply is crucial to understanding the behaviour of a narcissist and managing relationships with them.

Having a deep connection with someone is not a priority for a narcissist, nor is it something that a narcissist is capable of doing. People are seen and treated as pawns in the narcissist's game. The only time a narcissist will entertain 'changing' and will see a therapist, is when they have been ordered to by the courts, or when their marriage/relationship is about to end.

Attending therapy doesn't mean the narcissist genuinely wants help, and is prepared to work with the therapist to make changes. They usually will only go to show that they are cooperating, and the attendance is merely done to tick a box.

I believe that everyone has the ability to change – especially those who have narcissistic traits! The first step is wanting to, then for the second step, a daily consistent effort is required to move towards making any long-term changes.

Narcissism itself is nothing new, it dates back thousands of years. NPD officially became a recognised illness in 1980, this is when it entered the third edition of the *Diagnostic and Statistical Manual of Mental Disorders (DSM).*

Back in 1989 a leading psychiatrist and psychoanalyst, Glen Gabbard, recognised that not all narcissists fit the same mould and as a result then divided NPD into two subtypes: the Grandiose and the Vulnerable. Ever since that division was introduced, many leading experts have created further subtypes to allow for the diversities of today's society.

All of these subtypes present the same traits as someone who has NPD.

Understanding how these five subtypes work is important when you want to protect yourself against them. They all have their own distinctive patterns of behaviour and manipulation skill sets which they use to navigate and conquer their narcissistic world.

- **Grandiose (also known as agentic and overt)**
- **Covert (also known as closet or vulnerable)**
- **Communal**
- **Malignant**
- **Seductive**

All types of narcissists live their lives in patterns. It's these patterns you need to pay attention to when it comes to spotting a narcissist. Everyone lives their lives with distinctive patterns of behaviour and language when they communicate.

As a species, patterns are very important to our survival, you will know and understand these patterns as habits. Narcissists have a pervasive pattern of grandiosity, a constant need for attention and admiration and a complete lack of empathy. These patterns are displayed in both their behaviour and communication. More often than not, the moment you start to question if the person you are dealing with is a narcissist, is when the relationship appears to be very one sided – in their favour. This is the point when you may start to question if the person you are dealing with perhaps has a big ego.

Narcissists' communication styles will be very self-centred.

Narcissists will use language that reaffirms their perceived status in society. Often when you discuss someone else's success with a narcissist, they will very quickly flip it, diminishing that person's success and making the conversation all about them and their successes. Being 'happy' for someone else is near impossible for a narcissist. This grandiose pattern becomes very transparent when you find yourself always needing to defend the other person, and then eventually questioning if it's worth sharing others' successes and dreams with that person. You always end up feeling drained and perhaps a little confused because of the gaslighting after the conversation. This is an indication that the person you are dealing with has a very large ego.

A narcissist will communicate in a way that puts you in a position where you feel as though you should be in awe of this person (at all times!) and, at some level, are honoured to have a relationship with them. The way in which they communicate with you, will remind you of how important they are in your life. For them, it is crucial that they reinforce their superiority.

It is common for us to celebrate our achievements. In fact, it is important that we take time to recognise when we have accomplished something that requires hard work and focus. We need to feel proud of ourselves and celebrate our hard work. This is where it is very different for a narcissist. They will require praise and admiration on a daily basis for what you would consider to be everyday tasks. This is a need for them! Under no circumstances can they go without acknowledgement from you of their existence.

When it comes to having your first date with a narcissist, something they are highly likely to do is talk excessively about themselves, without showing much interest in getting to know their date. They are also likely to interrupt or dominate the conversation, and steer it back to themselves whenever it starts to focus on their date. Additionally, they may display a superficial charm or charisma that seems calculated to impress their date, rather than being a genuine expression of interest or affection. Overall, a narcissist on a first date may come across as self-centred and focussed on their own needs and desires, rather than being genuinely interested in their date.

The next few dates after the initial 'peacocking' phase will then be calculated to gather information from you which they can then use against you at a later date. They want information about your past, your ex, your family, your work, your hopes and dreams. And surprisingly enough when you are on a date with a narcissist you will find that you have also met someone who has the same background, hopes and dreams as you! This makes their victims feel as though they have met someone who truly understands them; thus the victim feels as though they have a connection with them.

If you don't, however, share all your information at a deep level with a narcissist, then they will quickly revert back to talking about themselves, this is due to boredom and out of habit.

The art of conversation with a narcissist is very low. Narcissists struggle to have a back-and-forth conversation because of the intense focus they have on themselves and their agenda, which is what makes it difficult for them to truly engage with others in a meaningful way. Narcissists prefer to keep conversations shallow and superficial in order to avoid feeling exposed or vulnerable.

People with big egos tend to have either no friends or family connections, or they have a rotating group of friends who often appear the same as them, and are highly competitive.

The only time a narcissist is interested in maintaining friendships is when that friendship will benefit them in some way, such as providing them with attention, admiration or social status.

Narcissists are prone to creating conflict and drama in their relationships, which is what leads them to falling out with friends or burning bridges. They are quick to feel offended or slighted by others, so often respond with anger, defensiveness or aggression to reaffirm their 'high' social status. Narcissists believe that others are jealous of them, which is why they will reinforce that certain 'friends' who are not playing ball with them are the ones who have the issue, and it is because of their friends' jealousy they are no longer friends.

This is important information when it comes to spotting a narcissist, as there will inevitably be a narrative that comes with their current connections or lack of! A narcissist moves through their life living in a web of lies. And this is one of the reasons it is difficult for them to have long-term relationships. They never want to be caught out on their lies so they need to keep people separate in order to never be exposed and to protect their ego.

This is controversial as I believe that narcissists are not entirely to blame for their behaviour. The reason those with big egos can get away with their toxic patterns of behaviour is because most people will make an excuse for them and the way in which they behave, which allows them to continue behaving as such.

We all have bad days, and people who have empathy and compassion understand that we don't always have good days, so acting out of character is acceptable on occasions. Those with empathy tend to create a narrative for the narcissist, which is what enables them to continue with their pattern of toxic behaviour. This gives the narcissist an excuse and permission for their big egos to continue with no boundaries or repercussions.

Cognitive dissonance is however something that a victim often develops from being in a relationship with a narcissist. This is an internal process where conflicting beliefs and attitudes are developed within the victim, as a result of being gaslighted by a narcissist.

Gaslighting:

- Involves manipulation and deception by another person
- Causes the victim to doubt their own perceptions and memories
- Can lead the victim to question their sanity or grasp on reality

Gaslighting is an external process that is done to the victim by another person's behaviour.

Cognitive dissonance:

- Involves conflicting beliefs, attitudes or values within oneself
- Causes discomfort or tension as a result of these conflicting beliefs
- Can lead to a change in beliefs, attitudes or behaviours in order to reduce the discomfort

Cognitive dissonance is an internal process that happens within a victim's mind.

Let me introduce you to Samantha who had experienced a narcissistic relationship with Tom for a few months, when she noticed that her thoughts and behaviour had started to change as a result of being in that relationship with him.

Samantha noticed that Tom would frequently belittle and criticise her for things that she felt were unfair or unreasonable. However, whenever she tried to bring up her concerns with Tom, he would dismiss her feelings and tell her she's being too sensitive.

Over time, Samantha starts to feel confused and anxious about their relationship. She loved Tom and wanted to make things work, but she couldn't shake the feeling that something was wrong. She began to doubt her own perceptions and memories, and started to feel like she was losing her grip on reality. This feeling was as a result of Tom's gaslighting behaviour.

Samantha experienced several common signs of cognitive dissonance, including:

- Feeling uneasy or conflicted about her relationship with Tom
- Struggling to reconcile Tom's behaviour with her own beliefs and values about what a healthy relationship should look like

- Trying to minimise or rationalise Tom's behaviour, even when it was hurtful or abusive
- Feeling like she was "walking on eggshells" around Tom, constantly trying to avoid saying or doing things that might trigger his criticism or anger
- Struggling to make sense of her own feelings and emotions, and feeling like she was losing touch with her own identity

These are all common signs of cognitive dissonance that can arise when someone has been gaslighted by a narcissist. It's important to recognise these signs and seek support from trusted friends, family members or mental health professionals to regain a sense of clarity and control over one's thoughts and feelings. Another tip is to write down each event, along with how it makes you feel as it happens. This will help you recognise if the person you are dealing with is toxic, become aware of their patterns and pay close attention to how they make you feel! These are the keys to spotting someone who has a big ego.

In the next chapter we will take a deeper look at the narcissist's toolbox of weapons.

5
The Narcissist's Toolbox

Narcissists have a set of skills which they have refined to ensure they are always satisfied.

The skills that I am referring to are:

- Gaslighting
- Belittling
- Blaming and shaming
- Silent treatment
- Manipulation
- Intermittent reinforcement

These are all forms of emotional manipulation which are designed to gain full control over their victims.

Gaslighting is the most damaging form of emotional manipulation as it makes the victim doubt their own memory, perception or sanity. It is a form of psychological abuse that can leave long-lasting emotional scars. The term originated from the 1938 play *Gas Light*, where the husband manipulates his wife by dimming the gas lights in their home and then denying that the lights were dimmed when she questioned him. Gaslighting can happen in various forms, including in relationships, at work or even within our own minds.

Gaslighting has developed and changed over the years and tends to be executed as a form of covert verbal abuse. This means you'll be highly unlikely to notice it as it won't be as transparent as what many of us know verbal abuse to be, which is shouting, swearing and using hurtful names to get reactions. Gaslighting is a learned behaviour that over the centuries has evolved and adapted to become an abuser's greatest tool. Many have started to speak up against obvious verbal abuse, and many now understand how this form of abuse can create so much damage. The damage that comes from being gaslighted works on two levels, the first is emotional and the second is mental/psychological. This is why gaslighting has such a profound effect on people, because ultimately it gives the abuser the power to create a new reality for you – which is their reality!

When you've been subjected to emotional abuse, the abuser will then start to work on isolating their victims from their friends and family. This isolation allows the narcissist to gain more control, knowing that their victims will be feeling helpless and alone, thus fully dependent on the narcissist. Here are some ways a narcissist can successfully isolate their victims:

- **Undermining their victim's relationships:** A narcissist may belittle their victim's friends and family and make them feel like they are not good enough. They may also spread rumours or lies about the victim's loved ones, causing them to doubt their loyalty and trustworthiness.

- **Controlling their victim's communication:** A narcissist may monitor their victim's phone calls, texts and emails, making it difficult for them to communicate with their loved ones. They may also limit their access to social media or block their friends and family from their profiles.

- **Discouraging social activities:** A narcissist may discourage their victim from participating in social activities or attending family events, making them feel guilty or ashamed for wanting to spend time with their loved ones. They may also create conflict or drama at these events, making it uncomfortable for their victim to attend in the future.

- **Isolating their victim physically:** A narcissist may move their victim to a new location, away from their friends and family, making it difficult for them to maintain their relationships. They may also refuse to allow their victim to leave the house or go out without them, further limiting their social interaction.

• **Creating a dependence on them:** A narcissist may create a situation where their victim is financially or emotionally dependent on them, making it difficult for them to leave the relationship or seek help from their loved ones.

It's important to remember that these tactics are abusive and not acceptable behaviour in <u>any</u> relationship. Victims who have been successfully gaslighted will not recognise this as abuse often until after the event. They will likely feel anxious and guilty, but not understand why or what they need to feel guilty about, frequently crying because they feel so powerless to what they are feeling and their current situation.

Many often wonder how they could have fallen victim to such abuse, but narcissists tend to come across very confident when using this technique. This is why so many people fall victim to gaslighting. When someone is being gaslit they will believe they are stupid and incompetent, and feel inferior to that person, so assume that what that person is saying must be right.

Understand that there is a key ingredient that needs to be present for someone to be successfully gaslighted – and that ingredient is **TRUST**.

As humans we feel before we think. This natural human instinct is one which 'keeps us safe'. When we feel safe in someone's presence, we don't get triggered, and thus feel threatened, uncomfortable and not able to trust that person.

In the beginning of a relationship with a narcissist, they will work very hard to gain your trust, to make you feel safe, and appear to be someone who fully understands you. All these elements are crucial for the gaslighting to work. If a narcissist isn't successful in gaining your trust, their behaviour will change, and it will be done quickly. They will likely ghost you and move on to someone who is more malleable.

Gaslighting also happens in work environments. When a narcissist can't get you 'on their side' and trusting their every move, expect your time there to be made extremely difficult and for you to become the 'problematic employee'. The main reason you are such a problem is because you are perceived as a threat who could expose the narcissist. The narcissist will likely spread rumours in an attempt to undermine the victim's credibility, they will use tactics such as denying a promotion that was promised and manipulate performance evaluations, to make the victim feel isolated and regularly doubt themselves. I go into great detail around how to deal with a boss or work colleague like this in Chapter 13.

Gaslighting comes in various forms and it's not just narcissists who gaslight.

Firstly, not everyone who gaslights is a narcissist. This includes your friends, sometimes they can unintentionally gaslighting you.

Imagine you and your friend are having a conversation about a recent disagreement you had with a mutual friend. You feel upset and hurt about the situation, and you're looking for support and validation from your friend. But as you start to explain what happened, your friend interrupts you and says, "I don't remember it that way. I remember you being the one who started the argument."

At first, you brush it off, thinking that maybe your memory is faulty. But as the conversation continues, your friend keeps insisting that your version of events is inaccurate and that you're overreacting. You start to doubt yourself and your own perception of what happened. You begin to wonder if maybe you did start the argument and if you're the one at fault.

Your friend in this situation has gaslighted you, causing you to doubt your own perceptions, memories and sanity, not wanting to acknowledge your version of events. While this may not have been your friend's intention, their behaviour is still having the same negative effect.

There are a few reasons why someone might unintentionally gaslight a friend. One possibility is that they genuinely remember the situation differently and are simply trying to offer their own perspective. However, this can still be harmful if they're not acknowledging your feelings and dismissing your experience. Another possibility is that your friend may be uncomfortable with conflict or negative emotions, so they're trying to downplay the situation in order to avoid any further confrontation. They may also be trying to protect the mutual friend involved in the disagreement and don't want to acknowledge any wrongdoing on their part.

Regardless of the reason, it's important to recognise when someone is unintentionally gaslighting you and you must be prepared to take steps to address the situation by making your friend aware of how they have made you feel.

It is very difficult for victims of narcissistic abuse to recognise when they are being gaslighted. Second guessing their perceptions of reality and doubting their ability to understand situations, would have become second nature to them. So, when friends and loved ones unintentionally gaslight them they assume that what they are saying is the truth and as a result stay stuck in that constant cycle of doubt and self-blame.

Here are some phrases that could unintentionally gaslight a victim of narcissistic abuse:

1. "Are you sure that's what happened?"
2. "You're overreacting, you do tend to do that."

3. "It couldn't have been that bad, you always end up going back."
4. "I don't remember it that way."
5. "You're being too sensitive."
6. "That's not what I said/did."
7. "You must have misunderstood/misinterpreted the situation."
8. "You're always making a big deal out of everything."
9. "Why do you always play the victim?"
10. "You're just being paranoid."

Friends and family members need to listen to and support victims of narcissistic abuse when they share their stories, and avoid invalidating their experiences or making them doubt their perceptions of reality. If it is something that makes you feel uncomfortable, express that, and then suggest they speak to a professional who specialises in this field and can give them the support they need.

Parents are gaslighters too!

Parents have also been known to unintentionally gaslight their children by denying that a traumatic event from the victim's childhood ever happened. This is a common occurrence and is something that parents need to be aware of. I want to share this story with you about a woman I am going to call Emma and the impact her parents' gaslighting had on her.

Emma had always been a sensitive child. She had a tendency to worry about things that others her age didn't, and sometimes her parents found her behaviour frustrating. When she was around ten years old, she experienced a traumatic event that left her feeling scared and vulnerable. One evening, as Emma was getting ready for bed, she tried to tell her parents what had happened. She told them about how she had been walking home from school when a man in a car had started following her. She remembered feeling scared and running away, but the man had eventually caught up with her, grabbed her but she managed to get away.

Emma's parents listened to her story, but instead of comforting her, they dismissed her experience. Her father told her that she was probably mistaken, that she must have misinterpreted what had happened. Her mother told her not to be silly, that she was just imagining things. Emma felt confused and hurt. She knew what had happened to her, but her parents were making her doubt her own memory.

As Emma grew older, she developed numerous mental health disorders and began to realise that her parents had been gaslighting her. They had been manipulating her memory and perception of the traumatic event, making her doubt her own experience. As a result of this, Emma felt confused, anxious, and deeply insecure. Emma's parents had gaslighted her in several ways. First, they denied the reality of the event. By telling her that she must have imagined it or misunderstood what had happened, they made her doubt her own memory. Second, they invalidated her feelings. By dismissing her experience and telling her not to be silly, they made her feel like her emotions were unimportant. Third, they minimised the impact of the event. By downplaying what had happened, they made her feel like it wasn't a big deal, which added to her confusion making her feel even more alone, as for Emma, this had deeply disturbed her. Emma's parents had unintentionally gaslighted her because they didn't understand the impact of their words and actions. They had thought they were helping her by reassuring her that everything was okay and no harm was done, but in reality, they were causing her more harm.

Gaslighting is especially damaging in family relationships because it can create a sense of confusion and mistrust. Children who are gaslighted may feel like they can't trust their own parents or family members, which can cause long-term damage to their emotional well-being. If you are a parent or caregiver, it's important to be aware of the impact your words and actions have on your child. Here are some tips to help you avoid unintentionally gaslighting your child:

1. **Listen to your child:** When your child is expressing their feelings or recounting an experience, listen to them with an open mind. Avoid dismissing or minimising their emotions, and try to validate their experience. Children have a hard time expressing emotions and can't always clearly express how they feel, so it is important to be patient with them when they are trying to open up.

2. **Believe your child:** If your child tells you that something has happened, believe them. Don't dismiss their experience or make them doubt their own memory. Asking them if they are sure if that's what happened, can trigger them into feeling as though you don't believe them and this will shut them down even further as a result. Instead get curious and ask questions to fit the pieces of the puzzle together.

3. **Avoid blaming your child:** If your child has experienced a traumatic event, avoid blaming them for what happened. Instead, focus on supporting them by letting them share whatever they feel comfortable with and help them feel safe by not overreacting.

4. **Seek help:** If your child has experienced a traumatic event, it would be wise to seek help from a therapist or other professional. You are only human and not everyone has the capacity to deal with traumatic events. Seeing a professional can provide support and guidance for both you and your child.

While up until this point it would seem like gaslighting is only associated with external sources, such as abusive partners, parents, friends and co-workers, understand that we can also gaslight ourselves.

Self-gaslighting makes you believe that you are the problem!

Self-gaslighting can be particularly damaging because it can also make it harder to recognise and address external gaslighting, as we may be more likely to believe that we're the problem rather than the abuser.

Self-gaslighting can occur due to a variety of reasons, but often it is a defence mechanism employed by individuals who are afraid to face the truth about themselves or their situation. For example, a person who is struggling with addiction may engage in self-gaslighting to justify their behaviour and convince themselves they don't have a problem. They may tell themselves that they can quit at any time or that they only drink or use drugs to manage their stress.

Another common reason someone may learn to self-gaslight is due to past traumas or experiences. If a person has experienced abuse or neglect in their childhood and were gaslighted, they may learn to doubt their own memories and perceptions as a way to cope with the trauma. They may tell themselves that the abuse wasn't that bad or that it didn't happen at all. This behaviour can become so ingrained that they continue to do it long after the traumatic event has passed. This is typically why people end up in a toxic relationship because their traumatic experiences in childhood have left them an imprint of what a 'normal/healthy' relationship looks like. Those who grew up in this environment may also learn to suppress their own needs and desires in order to avoid conflict, leading to difficulty setting boundaries and standing up for themselves later in life.

Additionally, societal pressures and expectations can contribute to self-gaslighting behaviour. For example, if a person has been told their whole life that they are not good enough or that they are worthless, they may begin to believe these messages and gaslight themselves. They may tell themselves that they don't deserve happiness or success and that they are destined to fail, so they often back away from new experiences and become a victim to the beliefs of others.

It is possible for someone to change their self-gaslighting behaviour, but it requires a willingness to confront the truth about themselves and their situation. This can be a difficult and sometimes a painful process, but it is essential for personal growth and healing.

Here are some steps that someone can take to stop self-gaslighting:

1. **Acknowledge the behaviour:** The first step in changing self-gaslighting behaviour is to recognise that it is happening. This may involve becoming more aware of the negative self-talk and questioning one's own perceptions.

2. **Challenge negative self-talk:** When negative self-talk arises, it is important to challenge it and ask oneself if it is really true. This can involve examining the evidence and considering alternative explanations.

3. **Seek support:** Changing self-gaslighting behaviour can be a challenging process, and it is important to have a support system in place. Confide in a trusted friend or family member who you know won't gaslight you to support you on this journey.

4. **Practise self-compassion:** Learning to be kind and compassionate to oneself is essential for overcoming self-gaslighting behaviour. This involves treating oneself with the same kindness and understanding that one would offer to a close friend.

5. **Seek professional help:** If self-gaslighting behaviour is causing significant distress or interfering with one's ability to function, it may be helpful to seek professional help.

If someone does not rectify their self-gaslighting behaviour, it can have significant long-term consequences. The constant self-doubt and questioning of one's perceptions can lead to chronic anxiety and depression, as well as difficulty forming and maintaining relationships. It is not uncommon for someone to also experience physical effects, such as headaches, sleep disturbances and digestive issues. In extreme cases, self-gaslighting can contribute to the development of personality disorders and other mental health conditions.

Many who have been in a toxic relationship self-gaslight as a defence mechanism designed to protect themselves from the truth, or the reality of the situation. It is possible to change this behaviour by following the steps above and getting any help or support you need.

Why does a narcissist block and ghost someone?

Blocking and ghosting is another tool that is often used by narcissists as part of the tactic of intermittent reinforcement. Intermittent reinforcement is a pattern of reward and punishment that is unpredictable, inconsistent and therefore highly addictive. It is commonly used by abusers and manipulators to keep their victims emotionally hooked and dependent on them.

In the case of a narcissist, they will use blocking and ghosting as a way to provide intermittent rewards (i.e., attention, validation, love) followed by intermittent punishments (i.e., rejection, abandonment, silence). This creates an emotional rollercoaster for the victim, who may feel elated one moment and devastated the next.

When a narcissist blocks and ghosts someone, they are essentially cutting off the supply of attention and validation that the victim has become dependent on. By suddenly withdrawing, and implementing the silent treatment, this can be extremely distressing and confusing for the victim, as they may not understand why they are being ignored or rejected. However, just as suddenly as they withdrew, the narcissist may also reappear, showering the victim with affection and attention once again. This intermittent reinforcement is highly addictive as the victim may cling onto the hope that things will go back to the way they were before.

Over time, the victim becomes conditioned to expect the sudden highs and lows of the relationship, and may even begin to associate the pain and anxiety of being blocked and ghosted with the pleasure and excitement of being reunited. This is the reason many feel addicted to their abuser as this can create a powerful cycle of addiction and dependency, with the victim becoming trapped in a pattern of seeking validation and approval from the very person who is causing them harm.

It is important to recognise that this cycle of intermittent reinforcement is not a sign of love or healthy relationship dynamics. It is a manipulative and abusive tactic that is intended to keep the victim trapped and powerless. If you are in a relationship with a narcissist who is using blocking and ghosting as part of their manipulation game, take the message that they don't love you and it is time to remove them from your life.

You'll never be good enough – for a narcissist!

When the narcissist is successful in their emotional manipulation, feeling like you are never good enough, and whatever you do for the narcissist is never good enough, will become a way of life for you. Belittling is almost a second language for a narcissist, the constant put downs ensure the victim feels small and insignificant. Narcissists will often criticise their victim's appearance, intelligence or abilities, or they may make fun of the victim in front of others. Belittling will make victims feel worthless, eroding their sense of self-esteem and self-worth.

Narcissists will regularly shift the blame of their actions onto the victim. They want the victim to feel like they are responsible for the abuser's behaviour so they may use guilt-tripping tactics to make the victim feel like they are at fault. Blaming enables narcissists to strip away a victim's boundaries, making it difficult for them to stand up for themselves.

Infidelity is common when you're in a relationship with a narcissist, and they will often blame their victim for their infidelity, using guilt-tripping tactics and criticism of their victim's appearance:

"I cheated on you because you've let yourself go. You used to be so fit and attractive, but now you've gained weight and stopped taking care of yourself. I just couldn't stay attracted to you anymore. It's not my fault, it's yours for not taking care of yourself."

In this example, the narcissist is using the victim's appearance as a way to shift the blame onto them for the narcissist's infidelity. By criticising the victim for gaining weight they are able to intensify the impact of their emotional manipulation. First by making the victim feel responsible for their own betrayal, and second, they also lower their victim's self-esteem and confidence. This is an easy get-out clause for narcissists as it ensures they don't have to take ownership of their actions. The narcissist knows that once they gain full control over their victims, they will feel powerless and helpless, as a result they will be unable to assert their own autonomy and independence.

The power of triangulation

Narcissists use triangulation as a way to gain power and control over their victims. They thrive on the drama and conflict they create, and they are always looking for ways to manipulate those around them. They are skilled at convincing their victims they are the only ones who can be trusted, creating a sense of dependency and loyalty that makes it difficult for their victims to break free from their control.

There was a woman named Lily, who was smart, confident and beautiful, and she knew it. Lily was a narcissist. She loved attention and admiration from others. She was always looking for ways to make herself look good, and she didn't care who she hurt in the process.

Lily had two close friends, Sarah and Emma. They had been friends since they were teenagers and had shared many experiences together. However, Lily was always jealous of their friendship, and she felt like she was being left out. She wanted to be the centre of attention and didn't like it when her friends spent time together without her.

One day, Lily decided to start using triangulation as a way to control her friends and manipulate them. She would tell Sarah things about Emma that weren't true, like how Emma had talked behind her back or how she had been spreading rumours about her. Sarah believed Lily, and she started to distance herself from Emma.

At the same time, Lily would tell Emma things about Sarah that weren't true, like how Sarah had been talking about her behind her back or how she was trying to sabotage her relationship with her boyfriend. Emma believed Lily and she started to distance herself from Sarah.

Lily enjoyed watching her friends fight and compete for her attention. She loved being the one they turned to for advice and comfort. She would listen to their complaints and tell them what they wanted to hear, even if it wasn't true.

As time went on, Sarah and Emma became more and more distant from each other. They would avoid each other at social events and barely spoke when they did run into each other. Lily loved it. She felt like she had all the power and her friends were just pawns in her game. However, Lily's game eventually caught up with her. Sarah and Emma both started to realise that they had been lied to and manipulated by Lily. They confronted her about it, but she denied everything and blamed them for the problems in their friendship.

In the end, Sarah and Emma decided to end their friendship with Lily. They realised that they couldn't trust her and that she would always put herself first, even if it meant hurting others. They were both hurt by the experience and it took them a long time to heal from the damage that Lily had caused.

Triangulation can cause people to lose trust in not only themselves but also each other, questioning their own judgement, leaving them feeling isolated and alone. Narcissists like Lily have a history of lying, speaking negatively and manipulating others, they don't care about the damage they cause to others as long as they get what they want.

Always pay attention to the facts and trust your instincts. Listen to your gut when it comes to dealing with people who seem too good to be true.

The narcissist's ultimate defence mechanism – projection!

Projection is a defence mechanism that is often used by narcissists to protect their fragile ego and self-esteem. In this mechanism, the narcissist projects their own unacceptable thoughts, feelings and traits onto another person, often blaming them for their own inadequacies or mistakes. This allows the narcissist to maintain their self-image as perfect, superior or faultless, while shifting the blame or responsibility onto someone else. When a narcissist projects onto someone else it makes them feel better about themselves.

Projection is a common tactic that can be difficult to detect and confront. It can cause a great deal of harm to the person on the receiving end, leading to confusion, self-doubt and even feelings of guilt or shame.

What is projection?

Projection is a psychological defence mechanism that involves attributing one's own unacceptable thoughts, feelings or behaviours to someone else. It is a way of denying or disowning one's own negative qualities, often by projecting them onto others. For example, a narcissist who is jealous of someone else's success may accuse that person of being jealous of them. In this way, the narcissist avoids acknowledging their own feelings of envy and insecurity, and instead, turns the tables and makes the other person responsible for the negative emotions. They are hoping that perhaps that person will start to tell the narcissist that they are indeed successful and downplay their success at the same time.

I would like to point out that projection is not unique to narcissists and can be used by anyone as a way of coping with uncomfortable or conflicting emotions. However, narcissists are particularly prone to using this mechanism because of their deep-seated insecurity and need for validation. By projecting their negative qualities onto others, they are able to maintain their perfect, superior image!

How do narcissists use projection?

Narcissists use projection in various ways, here are some examples:

- When projecting their own flaws and faults onto their partners, colleagues or family members, this causes them to feel guilty or ashamed. For example, a narcissistic parent may blame their child for their own shortcomings, criticising them for not living up to their expectations, they want to make their child feel responsible for their own failures.

- Narcissists may also use projection as a way of deflecting criticism or blame. When confronted with their own mistakes or flaws, they may deny responsibility and instead accuse others of the same wrongdoing. For example, a narcissistic boss may blame their employees for the company's failures, rather than taking responsibility for their own poor decisions or leadership.

• Projection can also be used as a way of gaslighting, or manipulating someone into doubting their own perceptions or reality. Narcissists may project their own negative emotions onto their partners, causing them to question their own sanity or judgement. For example, a narcissistic partner may accuse their significant other of being overly emotional or paranoid, when in fact, they are the ones who are acting irrationally or unfairly.

Being on the receiving end of projection can be very damaging to your self-esteem and mental health. Which is why it is important to recognise it.

Projection can lead to confusion, self-doubt, and feelings of inadequacy or guilt.

When someone is constantly blamed for things they did not do, or accused of having negative traits they do not possess, it can be difficult to maintain a sense of reality or self-worth.

Imagine a couple, Johnathan and Marie. Johnathan is a narcissist who frequently uses projection to avoid taking responsibility for his actions. One evening, Johnathan forgets to pick up Marie from work, leaving her stranded at the office. When Marie confronts him about it, Johnathan becomes defensive and accuses her of being too demanding and controlling. In this situation, Johnathan is projecting his own feelings of guilt and inadequacy onto Marie. Instead of acknowledging his mistake and apologising, he is shifting the blame onto her and making her feel responsible for his actions. This causes a breakdown in communication, as Marie is unable to have an honest conversation with Johnathan about the issue. She may become defensive or shut down, leading to further conflict and resentment in the relationship.

Over time, these patterns of projection and defensiveness can erode the trust and intimacy in the relationship. Marie may begin to doubt her own perceptions and feelings, feeling as though she is always the one at fault as she is too demanding. She may also become less willing to share her thoughts and feelings with Johnathan, fearing that he will invalidate or dismiss them. Projection can lead to a breakdown in communication and relationships, making it difficult for both parties to maintain a healthy and fulfilling connection. Maintaining a connection with a narcissist is very difficult, and dare I say, impossible, as they don't have the ability to create healthy connections.

Let's take a look at the different types of narcissists.

6
Type One: The Ultimate Narcissist

Grandiose is what you may call the 'ultimate' narcissist. They are by far the most transparent group of narcissists and these are the types who immediately come to mind when a 'narcissist' is mentioned.

The grandiose narcissist is often perceived as a very successful individual. They may be a leader, a CEO of a company or a public figure with many adoring fans. Research has shown that grandiose narcissism is more prevalent in certain professions. It is crucial to acknowledge that not all individuals in these professions possess unhealthy narcissistic traits; however, these fields tend to allure people who exhibit characteristics linked with grandiose narcissism. As a result, these professions have been found to have a higher incidence of grandiose narcissism:

- CEO/executive level positions: Individuals in leadership positions often have a strong desire for power, influence and control, which can be appealing to those with grandiose narcissistic traits.

- Law enforcement: The high-stress, high-stakes nature of law enforcement can attract individuals with a strong sense of self-importance and a need for admiration.

- Politics: The world of politics is highly competitive and often requires individuals to present themselves as confident, powerful and capable. These traits can be appealing to those with grandiose narcissistic tendencies.

- Entertainment industry: The entertainment industry is known for attracting individuals with larger-than-life personalities and a need for attention and validation.

- Sales: Sales professionals often rely on their ability to charm and persuade others to make a sale. Grandiose narcissists may be attracted to this profession because it allows them to use their charisma to manipulate and control others.

It's important to note that these professions are not inherently negative or bad. However, when individuals with grandiose narcissistic traits hold positions of power or influence, it can lead to unethical behaviour and a lack of concern for the well-being of others. It's important for organisations and individuals to be aware of the potential for narcissistic behaviour in these professions and to take steps to prevent it from causing harm.

Grandiose narcissists firmly believe that they are without a doubt a special, unique and superior person who is above everyone else, and they are not afraid to show it. The problem is, these people don't know how to feel good about themselves without being at the epicentre of attention. This inherent need for attention can be exhausting for their supplies, which is incredibly frustrating for the narcissist and is a reason they have so many avenues and people lined up to ensure they always get their supply.

These types of narcissists tend to be extroverted and assertive, they will appear overconfident and competent, and they will also show a huge dislike towards 'fellow' experts in their fields. Grandiose narcissists also think of themselves as so intelligent no one could ever know more than them. Their reiteration of this belief is an obvious narcissistic pattern that shouldn't be ignored.

These types of narcissists fall into the overt type category, because they're haughty behaviour can so easily be observed by others, they often show up as the 'big' person in the room who's thirsty for compliments. When faced with a threat – usually someone who can see through them – grandiose narcissists will display unusual amounts of vindictiveness and rage in order to intimidate 'the threat' and put themselves back in a position of power.

Here are the signs of a grandiose narcissist:

- Envious of others and thinking that others are envious of them
- Appearing arrogant, conceited or self-absorbed
- Believing they are so special that they can only associate with other 'special' people
- Having zero care, compassion and empathy for others
- A desperate need for admiration
- An exaggerated sense of importance
- Fantasies of power and increased success
- An expectation of special attention, treatment and gifts
- Taking advantage of others to fulfil their goals
- Very quick to anger if anyone contradicts or disagrees with them
- Being boastful, frequently bragging about their achievements

A grandiose narcissist is by far the easiest to spot, especially when it comes to dating. They will initially be super charming and charismatic. Their dating profile will be one that screams *look at me!* with self-indulgent, vain pictures and taglines that are boastful and pretentious. The tag lines will likely say things like, *I can get any man I want*; *I don't need you, it's you who needs me! ;)*; *You're lucky you met me, I'm about to change your life ;)* The perceived playful wink face at the end is added to lighten the mood. Being blatantly arrogant is too easy for this narcissist, so that winky face ensures that they make you smile and you of course understand the message, the message that they are not only better than anyone else but that they are also flawless.

Their communication style will be boastful, they want you to know that the person you are entertaining is one of high status and is highly sought after. They will want you to feel 'lucky' that you are talking to such an amazing person – this is so that you can really show your admiration and appreciation for the connection.

The questions that they will ask you are executed with the intent of you asking them the same thing back so they have an opportunity to once again shine! If you don't ask them the same question back, they will pull you up on not asking with a sarcastic comment like "oh so you're really not interested in me then seeing as you didn't ask 'X'"

This comment is made with the intention that you will then definitely ask them, and if you don't, they will become offended and will show signs of sulking.

They will show a sense of pride when mentioning how others are jealous of them, they really do believe this to be the case and take it as a form of flattery. Usually this is also around the time when they will mention how incredibly possessive their ex was. They will mention this fact because they want you to realise they really are special and a highly-sought-after catch. Partners for a grandiose narcissist are treated like an accessory, they are there to make the narcissist look good!

They will expect you to chase them, and their style of communication ensures that you do this. If you don't, they will move onto their other dating prospect. Understand that this type of narcissist needs to be entertaining a few prospects to keep their ego boosted. Nothing will change this behaviour, not marriage or children. Having numerous 'supplies' forms part of this powerful narcissist's identity.

Social Media has become the perfect playground for a grandiose narcissist.

The day a grandiose narcissist was introduced to social media was the day their appetite for attention and validation became insatiable!

Narcissists have always sought out supply from others, even before social media existed, and this was a bit of a task that required a fair amount of effort. Since social media came along, narcissists have 'free range' supplies who they can reach in the comfort of their own homes, using minimal effort.

Narcissists love to use social media as a platform to showcase their idealised self-image and gain a group of adoring fans who are always there ready and waiting to be a supply when they are called upon.

Here are some ways social media has impacted the supply of a narcissist:

- **Constant validation:** Social media provides a constant stream of validation and attention for narcissists. They can receive likes, comments and followers on their posts, which can be a significant source of validation for their grandiose self-image.

- **Image crafting:** Narcissists can use social media to craft an idealised image of themselves. They can carefully curate their posts to make themselves appear more successful, attractive and popular than they actually are, thus getting attention and validation for their fantasy lifestyle.

- **Manipulation:** Narcissists can use social media to manipulate their followers and gain control over them. They may use tactics such as love bombing, gaslighting and triangulation to control their followers and get the attention they crave.

- **Comparison and envy:** Grandiose narcissists can't help but compare themselves to others and feel envious of their success or popularity. This comparison fuels their need for attention and validation even further.

- **Online dating:** Narcissists may use online dating apps to find new sources of attention and admiration. They may use these platforms to manipulate and control their partners, often leading to toxic and abusive relationships.

Before the age of social media, narcissists often obtained their supply through in-person interactions, such as work, social events or dating. They would use their charm, charisma and manipulation tactics to gain control over their victims and obtain the attention and admiration they craved. Social media has also made it easier for narcissists to engage in love bombing, gaslighting and other manipulative tactics. They can use these tactics from a distance and manipulate multiple victims at once, without ever having to meet them in person.

In short, while narcissists have always sought out supply from others, social media has made it easier for them to do so on a larger scale, with more tools at their disposal, and with less accountability for their actions.

7

Type Two: Covert Narcissist – aka the Victim

Our covert narcissist is the one who often gets confused with someone who is deeply depressed. They present as someone who has a lot of anxiety and will appear to have a tough time fitting into the world with their unique struggles. I call these types 'the victim' simply because that is exactly how they come across. They have the same symptoms of NPD but often they hide the more obvious signs underneath the appearance that are suffering from anxiety and depression and are struggling to cope with life.

Covert narcissists will ooze self-pity, which is why playing the victim works so well for them, acting as a substitute for that lack of authentic self-worth. A covert narcissist will wear a mask that portrays them to have a very tough life. But don't be fooled by this 'victim mask' as covert narcissists are just as destructive as those with more overt narcissistic behaviours. While this type of narcissism is more difficult to recognise, as these types of narcissists tend to be more introverted and needy, they do use a distinctive weapon to satisfy their narcissistic needs. That weapon is passive aggression.

Passive aggression is a behaviour where an individual expresses their anger, resentment or frustration indirectly, often through subtle or manipulative means, rather than directly confronting the issue or person causing their negative feelings. This is great for a covert narcissist because they can express hostility or anger without appearing openly aggressive. This is very important as an obvious outburst could shatter their well-construed 'victim mask'. So, by using passive aggression they can avoid that mask slipping whilst still maintaining a level of control over others and avoiding direct confrontation.

Here are some examples of how a covert narcissist might use passive aggression:

- **Silent treatment:** Refusing to speak to the other person, ignoring them or giving them the "silent treatment" as a way for them to express their anger or frustration making the other person feel guilty, knowing that something is wrong.

- **Withholding affection or support:** Withholding affection, compliments or emotional support is used as a way to punish the other person for not meeting their needs or expectations.

- **Guilt-tripping:** Using guilt as a means of manipulation to make the other person feel responsible for their negative emotions or behaviours. You can never have negative emotions or behaviours around this narcissist, only they are allowed to have those feelings.

- **Indirect criticism or insults:** This is their favourite tactic, by using subtle or indirect means to criticise or insult the other person, such as making snide remarks, using sarcasm or making passive-aggressive comments they can boost their ego and, in their minds, lower your self-worth all in one hit.

Covert narcissists also love to be the first to point out any mistakes others make, but they will wrap it up in a way that makes them sound like it's really because they care. These types of narcissists will only target empaths because they know their sob stories will provide them with the perfect hook into an empath's deep compassionate nature.

Covert narcissists tend to claim that everyone around them hates them, especially their boss and work colleagues. According to this type of narcissist they are extremely talented and well versed in their profession, but no one can see it so they get bullied and will 'put up' with the bullying because that's the way life is for them. This gives the appearance that they have no control over what happens to them and how others treat them. But they will certainly have control over their partners and the attention that they receive, this is the one part of their lives that they absolutely do have full control over.

Here are the signs of a covert narcissist:

- Constantly seeking reassurance about their talents, skills and accomplishments
- Regularly blaming and shaming others
- Taking joy in creating confusion
- Procrastinating and disregarding
- Giving only with an intent to receive, expecting a lot of praise for the gift
- Not being emotionally accessible or responsive – but appearing to be

The covert narcissist often appears kinder and less obnoxious than their extroverted counterpart, which is often what throws people off believing that this person is indeed a narcissist. Covert narcissists tend to appear emotionally accessible. This type of narcissist is a master when it comes to displaying cognitive empathy. This developed skill enables the narcissist to put themselves in someone else's shoes/place to see their perspective. It is an unsympathetic response with a logical analysis of how they can appear to show empathy. This perspective that cognitive empathy gives has no true 'feeling' behind it. A covert narcissist uses cognitive empathy to complement their 'victim' appearance that they show to the world, making this the covert's greatest weapon when it comes to power play. This perfected performance is usually done with the intent to exploit or eventually leave the other person feeling small by disregarding, blaming or shaming them.

I want to introduce you to Chad, a manager at Costco, who is a talented musician and a keen runner who was looking for a partner who could complement him. One day, Chad met the partner he was seeking. Molly was a smart and attractive, kind-hearted woman who seemed outgoing and adventurous. They hit it off immediately and soon they were dating. At first, Chad was the perfect boyfriend, showering Molly with attention and affection. But as time went on, Molly began to notice that Chad had a few quirks that didn't quite add up. For one thing, Chad was constantly seeking reassurance about his talents, skills and accomplishments. He would often fish for compliments, asking Molly if she thought he was smart, talented or good-looking. Molly didn't mind at first, thinking it was just a harmless insecurity, but soon it became clear that Chad's need for validation was insatiable. No matter how much Molly praised him, Chad always seemed to want more. The times that she didn't he would respond in a passive-aggressive way.

Another issue was Chad's tendency to regularly blame and shame others. He would criticise Molly for small things, like not being organised enough or not having the right outfit for an event. He would also talk about his ex-girlfriends in a negative light, claiming that they were all "crazy" and that he was the victim in all his past relationships which is why he is struggling with his mental health. Molly found this behaviour unsettling, but she didn't know how to confront Chad about it. The last thing she wanted to do was upset him, so she decided to try and be the supportive girlfriend who would listen to what he had to say but not question him when he would share his past with her.

Chad also took joy in creating confusion. He would often make plans with Molly and then change them at the last minute, leaving her feeling frustrated and confused. He would also make contradictory statements, saying one thing one minute and then saying the opposite the next. This behaviour made it very difficult for Molly to know what Chad wanted or expected from her. But perhaps the most frustrating thing about Chad was his tendency to procrastinate and disregard important things. He would often forget important dates, like Molly's birthday or their anniversary, and then make excuses for why he didn't have time to plan something special. He would also procrastinate on important tasks, like paying bills or completing work projects, which would lead to unnecessary stress for Molly as he would expect her to pick up the slack, claiming that his mental health issues were causing him many problems.

Despite how Chad made Molly feel, she wanted to believe that he was a good person at heart and she convinced herself that his behaviour was just a result of his past experiences that have contributed to him having mental health issues, or he is struggling because of his busy schedule. You see, according to Chad, he had the most horrendous childhood, which was so bad he couldn't bear to talk to anyone about it. And he had always been unlucky in love with everyone he met taking advantage of him. So, Molly would often put her feelings to the side, despite feeling incredibly hurt and upset, coming to the conclusion that he didn't intentionally want to hurt her and if she could level up, then this would be what he needs to heal and change.

But one incident changed everything.

It was Molly's birthday. Chad had promised to take her out to a fancy restaurant for dinner. Molly was excited, looking forward to a night of romance and celebration. She had brought a new outfit and got her hair done especially for the occasion. But when Chad arrived to pick her up, he looked scruffy and was empty-handed. He hadn't even purchased her a card, let alone a gift. When Molly asked him about it, Chad brushed it off, saying that he had been too busy with work. Molly was hurt and disappointed. She couldn't believe Chad had disregarded such an important occasion, especially after he had promised to make it special. She tried to talk to him about it, but Chad became defensive, accusing her of being too materialistic and shallow. That was when Molly realised Chad was not emotionally accessible or responsive, despite his outward appearance. He only cared about himself and his own needs, and he believed that everyone else was to blame for his own faults and behaviours.

Covert narcissists have a tendency to monopolise every situation by turning the focus onto themselves and their supposed struggles in life. This behaviour serves as a means of control over their victims as they have conditioned them to always show respect and consideration towards their perceived difficulties, lest they make things "worse" for them. By playing the victim and garnering sympathy and attention, covert narcissists can maintain their grip on their victims and continue to manipulate them to their advantage.

8

Type Three: Communal Narcissist – aka the Hero

This is the single most disruptive narcissist subtype that you will encounter!

Out of all the narcissists these are the ones that you are going to really like, and dare I say admire! I call these types 'The Hero'.

These types of narcissists hide in the wide-open space for everyone to see. They pride themselves on being pillars to the community, with a much-cherished and vocalised giving persona. They will likely grace our television screens, our magazine covers and even lead our countries into the modern age. Communal narcissists have also been shown to have a high PSM (Public Service Motivation), or proclivity for non-profit work, which ties in beautifully with their 'selfless' image. They get their desire for control satisfied, when their desire to help is received, appreciated and accepted.

Their altruistic mask shows them to be someone who is incredibly selfless, someone who lives to serve others and has nothing but pure compassion towards humanity. But scratch a little deeper and you'll find it's all about projecting an image in the name of power and superiority.

Like any other narcissist, the ego is king with the communal narcissist.

It's all about them, and they expect their followers to pay them tribute in order to have their deep need of admiration satisfied.

These individuals rarely slip up and lose their composure when they are in public and have eyes on them. They have an impressive ability to fake genuine care and connection.

This is why they rarely get found out. It might surprise you to hear that there's a strong possibility that out of all the narcissist types, this is the one you have most likely come in contact with and felt completely safe with.

Here are the signs of a communal narcissist:

- Over-exaggerating their knowledge
- Believing themselves to have extraordinary potential and capability
- Extreme dedication to specific charities or causes
- Only seeming to show concern for societal needs in public
- Coming across as a martyr
- Fixated around having a mission or a calling
- Focussed on hierarchies or self-inflicted politics

Communal narcissists will go out of their way to show up in settings that have a group of people who they believe could become their next set of adoring fans! At support groups they will be the ones to forcefully express their knowledge and be overly supportive to everyone in the group, offering unsolicited advice at every opportunity. They have a confident demeanour which implies that they are competent in all aspects of the area that they are showing up in as an expert, and they will expect a high level of appreciation to follow their over-supportive ways.

When a communal narcissist is part of a sports team, the first thing you will notice is their ability to become a coach as well as a team player. They will appear to be extremely helpful, giving others help on how to improve their skills. This is done presumably for the good of the team, but that is not the motive behind their helpful behaviours. They are, in fact, building a fanbase of people who will begin to see them as an expert and the 'go-to' person in this sport. Being the talk of the club is crucial for them to have their ego boosted!

Communal narcissists will also be very difficult to coach in group environments where they are not in charge. This is because they have a belief that they are already above everyone else and as a result, they don't need to listen to the coach or trainer. Success, they believe, can be achieved on their own without anyone else. The need for popularity and admiration, with displays of excessive helpfulness, are two behaviours which need to be shown consistently for this particular person to be a communal narcissist. Where this type of narcissist differs from others, is how they seek to get their validation. This comes from the praise and admiration they receive for the community service they give. Hence the name, communal narcissist.

Communal narcissists rarely expose themselves in public as they know that showing any narcissistic tendencies or rages will lose them the perfected altruistic image they fight to uphold. They do, however, have a tactic that they use when they believe someone is seeing past the mask, or when a person is not playing exactly by their rules. Communal narcissists unleash the arts of favouritism and exclusion to create a negative perception of that person. Then they can create a false narrative that works in their favour to ensure this person becomes removed from the group and is no longer a threat.

Out of all the different types of narcissists and their victims, the communal narcissist's victims tend to be the ones who suffer the most. Behind closed doors and out of the public eye these victims will be subjected to an immense amount of abuse. Knowing that their partner is much loved and well respected by the public, the victim will feel completely alone and isolated. This type of narcissist has a distinctive manipulation style which uses the admiration of their fans to confirm the victim really is the one with the problem. They have a way of turning their victim into a very quiet, unconfident person, who has developed a belief that they are 'crazy' and have many mental health problems. They believe that because of the narcissist's kind, caring nature they are staying with the victim out of pity and that person is expected to show gratitude as a result, which of course means obeying their every command.

Communal narcissists' victims find it difficult to tell anyone about the abuse. This is because of their partner's status in society and their brainwashed condition. Brainwashing is what causes victims to have no confidence in what they are currently dealing with. Articulating what they are experiencing is difficult for them. The victims believe anyone they talk to would find it hard to believe what they are saying is true. And unfortunately, there is an element of truth to this, as more often than not the victim will be told by others how lucky they are to have such an amazing partner by their side, which again confirms everything the narcissist has been saying to them; that they are great and the victim is the one with the issues. Victims will rarely leave, giving the appearance of a happy doting partner. This is ideal for a communal narcissist as this adds to their 'perfect', much-loved persona that they need to uphold in public at all times.

Occasionally they will make others (their followers) aware of their partner's mental health issues just in case the partner does pluck up the courage to talk to someone, they are ready to back up what the narcissist has said about the victim's issues which would diminish the conversation, thus preventing the victim from getting help.

Think of a communal narcissist, much like Dr Jekyll and Mr Hyde, operating with two distinct and contrasting personas. On one hand, they present a benevolent and altruistic façade, where they appear to care deeply about the welfare of others and actively seek to help those in need. But on the other hand, lies a darker side, characterised by a deep sense of entitlement, a need for adoration and admiration, which they achieve through manipulation and control.

9

Type Four: Malignant Narcissist – the Quintessence of Evil

A malignant narcissist is considered to be the most severe and dangerous type of narcissist. This type of narcissist achieves their goals by harming and abusing others. Those with malignant narcissism tend to have a darker side to their self-absorption. These individuals go out of their way to be highly manipulative and don't care who they hurt as long as they get their own way. They get all of their power and validation from the pain and hurt they cause to others.

The term "malignant narcissist" was first coined by the psychoanalyst and psychiatrist, Dr Otto Kernberg, in the 1980s. Kernberg used the term to describe a specific type of personality disorder observed in some of his patients characterised by extreme narcissistic behaviour combined with a lack of empathy and a tendency toward aggression and manipulation.

Kernberg's concept of malignant narcissism builds upon previous theories of narcissism, such as those developed by Erich Fromm and Sigmund Freud, but places a greater emphasis on the harmful and destructive aspects of this personality type. Kernberg's work has been influential in the fields of psychology and psychiatry, and the term "malignant narcissism" is now commonly used to describe individuals who exhibit extreme narcissistic traits along with antisocial or psychopathic behaviour.

One of the biggest reasons this type of narcissist is so dangerous, is because of the antisocial behaviour they present. They are paranoid, egocentric, have no empathy and a sadistic streak. Many experts see little difference between malignant narcissism and psychopathy.

Malignant narcissists tend to have a large circle of acquaintances but no real friends.

People are either in their inner circle or they are enemies. There is no in-between.

They are not able to form real connections with anyone and are always on the lookout for new "friends" to feed their ego.

Here are the signs of a malignant narcissist:

- Unable to handle criticism
- Seeing the world in black-and-white terms
- Only having 'friends' or enemies
- Enjoying leaving a great amount of pain, frustration and even heartache in their wake
- Being open about not caring about the pain they cause others
- Relishing in the pain they cause others finding it empowering
- Doing whatever it takes to protect themselves in any situation
- Monopolising conversations and/or mistreating those who they perceive as inferior
- Not apologising for hurting others unless it benefits them
- Actively taking advantage of others to get what they want

There is a correlation between psychopaths and malignant narcissists. Both get pleasure out of hurting other people with the pain and discomfort they inflict on others giving them satisfaction. They also share some similar traits and behaviours. Both psychopaths and malignant narcissists exhibit a lack of empathy and remorse for their actions and have a disregard for the feelings and needs of others. They also favour using manipulative and exploitative behaviour to satisfy their desire for power and control over others. However, there are also some important differences between psychopaths and malignant narcissists. Psychopathy is considered a subcategory of ASPD, but the two are not identical. Psychopathy is typically seen as a more severe form of ASPD, characterised by a lack of empathy, impulsivity and a disregard for social norms and rules. In contrast, malignant narcissism is a subtype of NPD that is characterised by a combination of narcissistic traits, antisocial behaviour and paranoid tendencies. While there is an overlap between these two disorders, not all psychopaths are narcissists and not all narcissists are psychopaths.

Malignant narcissists function at their best when they are in relationships that are filled with fear. Having a fear of them, and the potential consequences of what might happen should you not adhere to how they want you to live your life and behave in the relationship, is for them the ideal relationship. And the reality is that you should indeed fear them.

Let's say you have a friend named Emily who starts dating a man named Todd. At first, Todd seems charming and attentive, but over time, Emily begins to notice some troubling behaviours. First, Todd constantly belittles Emily and makes her feel like she's not good enough. He criticises her appearance, her job and even her interests. He does this in a way that makes Emily feel like she's the one who's being too sensitive or not able to take a joke. Second, Todd is extremely possessive and controlling. He wants to know where Emily is at all times and who she's talking to. He monitors her phone and social media accounts and accuses her of cheating on him if she talks to other men. Third, Todd uses sex as a weapon to control Emily. He demands she performs sexual acts that make her uncomfortable and refuses to take no for an answer. He makes her feel guilty for not wanting to engage in these acts, saying she's not being a good partner. He also uses this as an excuse to cheat on her with multiple women.

Finally, Todd is also violent and physically abusive towards Emily. He hits her, throws things at her and threatens her with even worse violence if she ever tries to leave him or doesn't do as she is told. He also isolates her from her friends and family, making her feel like she has nowhere else to turn.

In this example, Todd is exhibiting many classic traits of a malignant narcissist. He is using emotional manipulation, control and physical abuse to keep Emily under his thumb, using fear as the main driver. He does not care about her feelings or well-being and is only interested in using her for his pleasure and satisfaction. Because these types of narcissists struggle to control their temper, they want to appear 'normal' to the outside world, so having a partner who can be seen to be happy and loyal to them, allows them to portray that image.

A malignant narcissist knows no limits, and their high level of antisocial behaviour will be displayed in public without any real shame; this should not be ignored. Antisocial behaviour refers to any behaviour that causes harassment, alarm or distress to other people, or that damages property or the environment. While antisocial behaviour is not a specific criminal offence, certain types of behaviour displayed can be dealt with through civil or criminal law, depending on the circumstances. It is important to keep evidence of these behaviours should you need to take legal action in the future.

Reactive abuse

When an animal is trapped in a cage and feels threatened or scared, it may lash out and become aggressive in an attempt to defend itself. Similarly, when a victim of abuse feels trapped and powerless in a situation, they may resort to reactive behaviour as a way to defend themselves or express their feelings of anger and frustration. Just as the caged animal needs to be released from its captivity to stop its reactive behaviour, victims of abuse need to be freed from their abusive situations to overcome their reactive behaviour and heal from the trauma they have experienced.

Reactive abuse can sometimes happen when a victim of abuse responds with aggressive or violent behaviour, which may include yelling, screaming, pushing, hitting, or any other physical or verbal acts of aggression which are all out of character for this person.

Reactive abuse often occurs in situations where the victim feels trapped and powerless in their relationship with the abuser. They may feel like they have no other way to defend themselves or express their frustration and anger towards the abuser, especially if they have been gaslighted or manipulated into believing the abuse is their fault.

When a victim responds with reactive abuse this is due to the ongoing trauma that they have experienced, and they have reached a point where the victim feels like they have no other way to protect themselves or express their feelings towards the abuser. When someone is experiencing ongoing abuse, their sense of self-worth and self-esteem can be eroded, leaving them feeling powerless and trapped. This can lead to a sense of hopelessness and despair, which can fuel their reactive behaviour.

Often victims become more reactive and aggressive in an attempt to defend themselves or make their abuser acknowledge their wrongdoing as they are desperate for validation that they are indeed a victim.

Overcoming reactive abuse

Overcoming reactive abuse requires a multifaceted approach that involves addressing the underlying trauma and rebuilding a sense of self-worth and empowerment.

Here are some steps that can be taken to help overcome reactive abuse:

- **Seek professional help:** A therapist or counsellor can help you work through the trauma of abuse and develop coping strategies to help you manage your reactive behaviour. They can also help you address any underlying mental health conditions that may be contributing to your behaviour.

• **Build a support system:** Surround yourself with people who are supportive and understanding of your situation. This can include family members, friends or support groups for victims of abuse.

• **Set boundaries:** Establish clear boundaries with your abuser and stick to them. This may include limiting contact or cutting off contact entirely if it is possible to do so.

• **Practise self-care:** Taking care of yourself is essential in overcoming reactive abuse. This can include getting enough sleep, exercising regularly and engaging in activities that bring you joy and fulfilment.

• **Develop coping strategies:** Identify healthy ways to manage your emotions and express your feelings without resorting to reactive behaviour. This may include deep breathing, journaling or engaging in creative outlets.

• **Learn about healthy relationships:** Educate yourself about what healthy relationships look like and how they function. This can help you identify unhealthy patterns in your own relationships and work towards building healthier ones in the future.

• **Practise forgiveness:** Forgiveness is a powerful tool in healing from trauma. Forgiving yourself for your reactive behaviour and perceived 'mistakes' is the first step, and the only step that matters which will help you move forward and let go of the past.

In conclusion, reactive abuse is a complex issue that requires a compassionate and holistic approach to healing. By addressing the underlying trauma and developing healthy coping strategies, victims of reactive abuse can begin to rebuild their sense of self-worth and empowerment, and move towards a healthier and happier future, without the need to react in ways which are deemed unethical thus creating a disconnect from those around them.

10

Type Five: Seductive – aka the Euphoric Narcissist

This type of narcissist is what I like to call the 'euphoric' narcissist, for the simple fact that they have the ability to make you feel incredible… in the beginning that is!

While all narcissists go in hard to love bomb you during the initial phases of the relationship, these types of narcissists will give an impression they admire you and may even idolise you. The compliments they will give you will be exactly what you want to hear, and those compliments are very likely to be something you've missed hearing from a previous partner, which is what also makes their words so effective. They are overzealous with the use of compliments They love to be flirtatious, and will confidently ask sexual questions in order to get deep into your fantasies very early on in the relationship, to ensure they know all the right things to say to you, and then of course later they will carry them out.

These narcissists are extremely cunning, they know how to use their body language to get your admiration. They often use an excessive amount of touch to accelerate your infatuation and ensure that you become obsessed very quickly.

Signs of a seductive narcissist:

- Being very seductive, and moving what feels to be too fast in the beginning
- An excessive focus on sexual performance
- Seeking approval of their sexual performance
- Their style of lovemaking is often focussed on appearance and image

- Always making promises they can't or don't keep
- They are very hard to pin down
- Constantly putting you down
- Neglecting you after sex
- Infidelity, violence and sexual addiction

Seductive narcissists feel entitled to sexual experiences and partners. They view themselves as superior to others with a grandiose sense of their sexual prowess. They cannot be truly intimate and connect with someone on a deep level, instead they exploit their partners. After an initial courtship where they try to impress and please a partner, a seductive narcissist will insist that their partner caters to their needs, using sex and intimacy as an ongoing weapon of intermittent reinforcement. This type of narcissist needs you to be obsessed with them and their body/image. They want their victims to constantly think about them, even when they're not around. This type of manipulation will leave victims struggling to focus on other things and they will feel compelled to seek out contact with the narcissist.

Many who have experienced sex with a seductive narcissist claim that it is the best sex they have ever had. This comes as no surprise, as sex is used as a tool to impress, entrap and manipulate you throughout the relationship, but more so in the early stages when they are working on having you hooked on them to create the sexual addiction.

When it comes to sex or making love, it's about two people enjoying, pleasuring one-another. You know when you are dealing with a seductive narcissist as they will be trying very hard to give a virtuoso performance. It will seem like an act… because that is exactly what it is. I once had someone describe it to me as circus sex, which I can only assume at the time was considered a good thing!

When you're on the receiving end of a seductive narcissist's showmanship, you are also playing a role as well. The expected role from you, is to validate and confirm/worship what an impressive god the narcissist thinks they are. So yes, after the act you will most certainly be expected to give an immense amount of praise and thanks.

Most sexual narcissists will often feel bored when having sex with their partners after the love bombing phase is over. They will struggle to open up emotionally because they have used up all their cognitive empathy tactics early on, and now have none left. For them, it is all about enjoying the game of manipulation and seeing how much control they can maintain over someone.

Once the love-bombing phase is over, the seductive narcissist will begin to demand that you cater primarily to their own selfish needs. You will be "on-call" to satisfy their sexual desires and will be required to engage in sexual acts which only they enjoy. You will no longer be an individual with your own thoughts, feelings and priorities. You will exist merely to satisfy the narcissist. Your own needs will be dismissed and ignored. They will also make claims that you are infatuated with sex and have an addiction to sex. This is in fact their way of deflecting the reality of the situation which is: they are the ones who have a sexual addiction.

Sexual addiction

Seductive narcissists have a secret…

And that is the reason behind why they are able to keep up the high sex drive privado is because most of them will have an addiction to sex. This addiction is fuelled by a sense of entitlement and their complete lack of empathy which is what leads them to behave compulsively, take risks and be quick to manipulate in the early stages.

Here are some signs that you are dealing with a narcissist who has a sex addiction:

- **Objectification of others:** A narcissist who is addicted to sex will view other people primarily as objects to fulfil their sexual desires. They may not care about the feelings, needs or boundaries of others, and they will be willing to manipulate or coerce others to get what they want.

- **Compulsive behaviour:** Engaging in compulsive sexual behaviours such as masturbating excessively or seeking out anonymous sexual encounters is normal for a narcissist who has a sex addiction. They will feel a strong compulsion to seek out sexual experiences, even when it puts them at risk of negative consequences.

- **Grandiosity:** Narcissists have a grandiose sense of self-importance and this can extend to their sexual behaviour. They will feel entitled to sexual experiences and partners, and may view themselves as superior to others in their sexual prowess.

- **Lack of empathy:** A narcissist with a sexual addiction will show no empathy for others, including their sexual partners. They will use others for their own sexual gratification, without regard for the feelings or needs of the other person. Sex for them is merely an act, not a joint pleasurable experience to create a mutual connection.

- **Manipulation:** A narcissist with a sexual addiction will manipulate others to get what they want. They may use charm, flattery or coercion to convince others to engage in sexual behaviour with them, and may be willing to lie or deceive to achieve their goals.

- **Risk-taking behaviour:** A narcissist with a sexual addiction will engage in risky sexual behaviour, such as having unprotected sex with multiple partners or engaging in sexual activity in public places. They may be willing to take these risks despite the potential consequences, such as sexually transmitted infections or legal problems.

- **Lack of intimacy:** Despite their focus on sex, narcissists with a sexual addiction will have trouble opening up emotionally and will avoid vulnerability in relationships.

- **Negative consequences:** A narcissist with a sexual addiction will experience negative consequences as a result of their behaviour, such as relationship problems, financial difficulties or health problems. Despite these consequences, they may continue to engage in the same behaviours, unable to stop or control their addiction.

Leanne is a sexual narcissist who was a successful businesswoman who had a reputation for being a bit of a player. She would admit that she enjoyed the attention of men, and she was never short of offers for a night out or a casual hook-up. She always enjoyed the game of cat and mouse and the excitement of meeting someone new. She loved that intense sense of power she felt when she could make men desire and chase her and she wasn't at all shy when it came to expressing how attractive men and women found her.

One day, Leanne met Jake, a handsome young man who worked at a rival company. He was charming and witty, and Leanne was immediately attracted to him. She was on her best behaviour with Jake, and she made a point of getting to know him better to make him feel like he could trust her. Jake knew of her reputation, but she was able to convince him that she was at a point in her life where she was wanting something serious. Leanne was incredibly seductive and moved quickly to establish a sexual connection with him. She was always talking about how much she wanted him and how much she enjoyed being with him. Jake was swept off his feet. He felt like he had finally met the woman of his dreams.

Leanne placed an excessive focus on their sexual performance, always wanting to know if Jake was enjoying himself and seeking his approval of her own performance. There were times she would even ask him to score the sex afterwards. The first time she asked him this Jake thought she was joking and said, "Oh around a 6 or 7." Leanne was deeply offended and her whole attitude changed, she began to tell him what he needed to do in order to be better. Jake then understood that question was no joke and he would score her, and the sex 10s from then on to avoid getting berated. She also had an unusual style of lovemaking that was focussed on her appearance and image, wanting to be seen as the perfect sexual partner which was something Jake has never experienced before, this eventually made him feel uneasy as she would also expect the same level of perfection from him.

Once Leanne felt like she had "gotten" Jake, her behaviour shifted. She became hard to pin down, always making promises that she couldn't keep. She would often cancel dates at the last minute, saying that she was too busy with work or other commitments. She would constantly put Jake down, reminding him that she could have anyone she wanted and that he was lucky to be with her.

Leanne also began to neglect Jake after sex. She would often purposely roll over to have her back to him, refusing to cuddle him, then fall asleep immediately afterwards. Another tactic she would use would be to create an argument straight after so she could get up and leave without saying goodbye. Jake felt like he was being used, like he was just a toy for Leanne to play with and then discard when she was done. This knocked Jake's confidence, he really began to doubt himself and his sexual ability.

Jake had suspicions that Leanne was cheating on him as he was told a couple of times by colleagues that she had been seen getting close with someone in local bars, and those dates coincided with the times she had gone AWOL. Jake tried to confront Leanne about her behaviour, because he loved her, and he desperately wanted to make it work. But his attempts would always fall on deaf ears and Leanne would turn it around back on him. She would say that the issues in their relationship were all Jake's fault, that he was being too clingy, or that he was trying to control her which she wouldn't accept as according to her she was controlled in past relationships so she wouldn't let this happen again. Jake felt like he was going crazy, like he was losing his mind. Just when he thought he understood what the problems were, predominantly Leanne's behaviour, he would find himself once again going back over everything that he had or hadn't done which had caused the issues.

After nearly two years of back and forth, Jake realised that he couldn't continue the relationship. He had lost all of his confidence and felt like he was being emotionally and sexually abused, and deep down he knew that he deserved better. He ended things with Leanne and moved on with his life, determined to find someone who would treat him with the respect and love he deserved.

Narcissists love triangle

I spoke about the purpose of triangulation with friends in a previous chapter. Narcissists typically struggle with monogamy because of their insatiable need for attention and admiration. They crave constant validation and stimulation, and one person can never provide enough for them.

Many narcissists will use triangulation as a way to have their needs met. As narcissists have a tendency to view others as objects or possessions, rather than individuals with their own needs and desires, they feel entitled to multiple partners and see no issue with lying or manipulating to get what they want.

Terry was a charming and successful businessman who seemed to have it all. He had a long-term partner of eighteen years, Ruth, and they had four children together. Terry also had a long-term girlfriend in another county called Sam who he had been in a relationship with for eight years. Sam knew about the mother of his children, and she was told they hadn't been in a relationship for the past ten years so she didn't have any concerns about Ruth. Instead, she supported Terry in having a relationship with his children, believing that Terry and Sam were no longer together.

Terry was, however, a narcissist and a master of love triangulation. He would often travel for work which became his perfect blanket for being able to have relationships with both of these women, without either of them knowing he was in a relationship with them.

On many occasions Terry would tell one of them that he was working away on business when he was indeed seeing the other woman, spending time in lavish hotels or staying at their homes being waited on hand and foot. Terry knew he had full control over these women, and no matter what happened he could use his manipulation skills to ensure they never had the courage to leave him. But Terry's triangulation didn't end there with just these two women, he would regularly meet other women for sex, as he wasn't capable of having an emotionally-connected relationship. He needed these interactions to validate his desirability and to keep his ego boosted.

Terry was also dating a younger woman over a three-year period called Connie who he ended up getting pregnant. Once this happened Terry lost his cool demeanour and made it clear that Connie and the baby will no longer have anything to do with him. Connie was confused by his reaction so began to dig into his life (mainly for the purpose of child support) and she discovered the truth about the other women in his life Ruth and Sam.

Connie did know about these women but she was told they were exes and he hadn't been in a relationship with either of them for years. Connie reached out to them initially in a curious way to see if they could help her locate Terry for the sake of their child. It was then that all three women discovered the truth and his infidelity and love triangle was exposed.

All three women found out that Terry would treat them exactly the same, making sure they felt special, but also keeping them at arm's length. He would never fully commit to either one, claiming that his work and having time with his children needed to come first.

Once Connie found out the truth and Terry had made it very clear that he would never be a father to their child, she made the decision to walk away and raise their daughter on her own. Ruth and Sam, however, didn't have the strength at that time to walk away.

Ruth was an incredibly loyal person; she had given this man eighteen years of her life and four children. Terry had insisted to Ruth that Connie was a liar. He said he never had a relationship with Connie like she had tried to get Ruth to believe. Instead, it was a very short-term fling, which was a mistake. He claimed the reason he cheated was because he felt very unloved and neglected at home. He wanted Ruth to feel guilty – which she did. By blaming her for his actions he was able to take the heat off the reality of the situation, which is the fact that Terry is a liar and a prolific cheat. Terry claimed that Connie was a silly young woman who was desperate to trap him because he had money, and she just wouldn't leave him alone. Terry claimed that Connie would say anything she could to ensure Ruth would leave him so Terry could be with her.

This was the same story he told Sam, and with Sam also being someone who was an empath she felt guilty and responsible for his actions. Blaming herself she quickly embarked on an extreme fitness regime to lose weight. Ruth also did something drastic: she developed bulimia in an attempt to become super skinny.

Terry told both Ruth and Sam the same story about Connie. Making it clear that she and their child would never show up again as he was done with her, and he never wanted that child so it was her problem and not his. Both women accepted that Connie was gone and she was nothing more than a mistake, but they now both know that Terry had been in a relationship with the two of them for years and they wanted to know what he was going to do about 'the other women'.

Terry relished in this development having two women fight against each other for him made him feel so incredibly powerful. This love triangle had reached new heights, and now he had some new games to play. He continued to see both women the same as before when he was away 'working' or having 'father-son time' with his children.

He would take these opportunities to block and ghost them when he was with the other one, creating arguments using the other woman's behaviour as a reason they would argue.

Both Sam and Ruth were jealous of each other's relationship with Terry. Terry would constantly lie to each of them, making them both believe that they were trying to steal him off from the other. He used sex as a way to make them try harder for him, to prove their love to him.

Terry's behaviour started to take a toll on both Sam and Ruth. They both felt like they were in a competition for Terry's attention, and they were constantly anxious and on edge. Ruth lost an unhealthy amount of weight and Sam ended up in a deep depression.

Terry's behaviour caused irreparable damage to both Sam and Ruth. They were left feeling betrayed and used. It took them a long time to heal and move on from the pain that Terry had caused. Both wish they hadn't continued with the relationship after they found out the truth about Connie, but both had been emotionally manipulated for years by Terry, so having the ability to break away wasn't an easy option for either of them.

11

Why Victims Feel Stuck

"If they are really that bad then leave them!" This is Gaslighting at its finest.

Leaving a narcissistic partner is one of the most difficult and painful experiences a person can go through. The psychological trauma inflicted by a narcissist can leave their victim feeling trapped, helpless and unable to escape – even when they don't live with them. While it may be easy for an outsider to look in and wonder why the victim can't just leave, the reality is far more complex.

One of the key reasons it's so difficult for a victim to leave a narcissistic partner is because of the nature of the abuse. Narcissistic abuse is insidious, often happening gradually over time in a covert manner. The narcissist will use a variety of tactics to ensure the victim begins to doubt their own reality and question their own judgement, feeling as though they need the narcissist to give them direction.

Another reason why it's difficult to leave a narcissistic partner is because of the intense emotional attachment that exists between the two people. Narcissists are skilled at making their victim feel like they are the only one who truly understands them. They use love bombing, flattery and grand gestures to create a sense of intimacy and connection. The victim often feels like they have found their soulmate, and narcissists love to reinforce that belief to hide the warning signs of abuse.

This intense emotional attachment is also called a trauma bond

Trauma bonds are powerful emotional attachments that develop between a victim and their abuser, and they can be incredibly difficult to break, but not impossible! Understanding what trauma bonds are and how they are formed is an important step in breaking the bonds that keep you attached to an abuser.

Here are some key points to help understand trauma bonds:

• Trauma bonds are formed when an abuser creates intense emotional experiences that leave the victim feeling helpless, powerless and dependent on the abuser for validation and a sense of worth.

• The victim will come to associate these intense emotional experiences with the abuser and develop a deep attachment to them, even if the experiences are negative or harmful.

• The abuser reinforces this attachment by alternating between periods of kindness and love bombing, and periods of abuse and neglect. This creates a cycle of intermittent reinforcement, where the victim is constantly seeking validation and love from the abuser.

• Trauma bonds can be broken by recognising their existence. Seeking support from a therapist who specialises in breaking these bonds, it is possible to be free from the abuser. Also joining a well-managed support group which is run by qualified people and having support from trusted loved ones.

• Setting firm boundaries with the abuser is an important step in breaking a trauma bond. This may involve limiting contact or what I recommend: cutting off contact completely.

• The process of breaking a trauma bond can be difficult and is likely to invoke feelings of guilt, shame and grief. Prioritising self-care and self-compassion is essential throughout the process.

• Engaging in positive self-talk, practising mindfulness and finding healthy ways to cope with stress and anxiety are great strategies for accelerating the process of breaking the trauma bond.

If you are struggling to break free from a trauma bond, know that you are not alone. There are many factors which play a role in keeping you stuck in the trauma bond cycle. Fear of retaliation is one of the biggest reasons many struggle to leave their narcissistic partner. Narcissists often use fear as a tool to control their victim. They may threaten to harm the victim or their loved ones if they try to leave. They may also use the legal system or financial threats to keep the victim trapped in the relationship. Some types of narcissists (usually covert) will also claim that they will take their own lives if their victim does leave them. Finally, leaving a narcissistic partner can be challenging because of the trauma that the victim has experienced. Narcissistic abuse can leave lasting psychological scars and challenging mental health disorders such as anxiety, depression, insomnia and Post-Traumatic Stress Disorder (PTSD). The victim will struggle to trust others and will have difficulty forming healthy relationships in the future if they don't heal from their trauma.

Leaving a narcissistic partner is a process and not something that can be done overnight. It takes time, patience and support from loved ones to make the decision to leave and to follow through with it. Remember, the narcissist would have worked hard to isolate their victims from their friends and family so many don't have any support. When the victim does eventually build up the courage to leave them and starts to follow through on a plan they have created, that victim will face a new set of challenges. Narcissists hate 'failing' and when one of their supplies manages to 'escape' it is taken personally and they will set about a plan to either get them back or inflict more hurt and pain on them using the following methods.

Smear campaigns

Narcissists are notorious for starting smear campaigns against their victims. Often this is done online via social media channels but it also happens in person. Smear campaigns can happen during the relationship, or after the victim has left the narcissist. But why do narcissists engage in this behaviour? What are they hoping to achieve? And why do they love to make themselves look like the victim after they have been left by their victim?

One of the main reasons narcissists start smear campaigns is to maintain control over their victims. Narcissists thrive on power and control, and when their victim tries to leave or assert their independence, the narcissist will feel threatened. By spreading lies and rumours about their victim, the narcissist can damage their reputation and isolate them from their support network. This can make the victim feel helpless and more likely to return to the narcissist. Another reason narcissists engage in smear campaigns is to protect their fragile egos. Narcissists have an inflated sense of self-importance and a deep-seated fear of rejection or criticism. When their victim leaves them, the narcissist will feel a sense of shame or embarrassment. Shame is an overwhelming emotion for a narcissist, which they will seek to avoid by presenting themselves as the victim. By doing so, they shield their ego from potential embarrassment and absolve themselves of any responsibility for their actions. This behaviour can lead to the narcissist receiving sympathy and attention from those who believe their victim narrative, ultimately enabling their need for validation and admiration.

Narcissists also engage in smear campaigns as a form of revenge against their victims. When a narcissist feels rejected or abandoned, they will lash out in anger in an attempt to punish their victim. Smearing their victim's name is a way for the narcissist to get back at them for leaving or asserting their independence.

Another reason narcissists start smear campaigns is to maintain their false self-image. Narcissists often present a polished and perfect image to the world, but this image is built on lies and manipulation. When their victim leaves them, the narcissist will feel exposed and vulnerable. By painting their victim as the villain, the narcissist can maintain their false self-image and continue to deceive others which is of most importance to them. Exposure is not something they can handle, which is why they very quickly set about starting a smear campaign. It's important to note that some narcissists may not always be aware they are engaging in a smear campaign. To some narcissists, their lies and rumours may seem like the truth. They may genuinely believe their victim is a terrible person and that they are the real victim in the situation. This belief is often held by a vulnerable/covert narcissist.

Hurt people hurt people…

This saying only applies to those with narcissistic tendencies as most individuals do not intentionally hurt others as a result of their own pain. Keep this in mind when you are witnessing someone telling their story of abuse. Narcissists seek revenge and will engage in smear campaigns by sharing their victim's personal details with strangers online. For the narcissist, it is crucial that others are aware of their victim's identity, as this may lead to further harassment and stress for the victim, hindering their ability to recover. Seeking revenge is a weak and entitled response that perpetuates the cycle of hurt. Instead, individuals should focus on self-healing and personal growth to break the cycle of hurt. This involves taking responsibility for one's actions, communicating effectively and developing empathy towards others. Healing from hurt is a process that takes time and effort, but it is worth it in creating a happier and more fulfilling life for oneself and others.

So, what can you do if you are the victim of a narcissist's smear campaign?

The first step is to recognise what is happening and not engage with the narcissist.

Responding to their lies and rumours will only give them more power over you.

Understand that they are desperate to get a reaction from you because when they do get a reaction, that confirms they still have a place in your life, and they are still able to control you. It's also important to document any evidence of the smear campaign, such as screenshots of social media posts or messages. This can be useful if you need to take legal action or if you need to defend yourself against the narcissist's lies. Learn to shift your focus away from the smear campaign and onto building a support network of people who know the truth about you and who can offer you emotional support. Try not to get wrapped up in constantly talking about the narcissist and what they are doing as this will add to your pain and could potentially trigger you to get back in touch with them.

Engaging in a smear campaign to prove someone is a liar and a narcissist is one of the most counterproductive actions you can take. Responding to the accusations can play right into the narcissist's hands, as they thrive on eliciting emotional reactions that may undermine the credibility of their victims. Hence, it is vital to resist the urge to respond and avoid falling into the trap of a smear campaign. Remember, the narcissist seeks your attention and validation, which is one of the biggest reasons they started the smear campaign in the first place. So depriving them of it is the best way to avoid being caught up in their manipulative tactics.

Finally, it's important to remember that the smear campaign is not about you, it's about the narcissist and their need for control, revenge and a false self-image. By recognising this, you can start to let go of their toxic influence and move on with your life. Healing can only happen when you decide it is time to let them and their tactics go.

Flying monkeys

Flying monkeys are individuals who are recruited by narcissists to do their bidding.

They are named after the flying monkeys in *The Wizard of Oz*, who were sent by the Wicked Witch to do her evil deeds. In the context of narcissistic abuse, flying monkeys are often used by the narcissist to manipulate, control and intimidate their victim.

Flying monkeys can take many forms, such as family members, friends, co-workers or acquaintances. They may not be aware that they are being used by the narcissist, but there are some who will be complicit in the abuse. The narcissist will use their usual tactics such as gaslighting, guilt-tripping or love bombing to recruit and manipulate their flying monkeys, this is why they tend to appear and behave so loyally to the narcissist because they have been convinced that the victim is the real problem.

One of the main reasons flying monkeys are so damaging to victims of narcissistic abuse is that they add to the victim's pain and sense of isolation. The victim may already be struggling to escape the narcissist's control and to assert their independence. When the narcissist recruits others to do their bidding, the victim may feel as though they are fighting a losing battle. They may also feel as though they are being punished for trying to leave the narcissist, or that they are somehow responsible for the abuse they are experiencing.

Flying monkeys can also be damaging because they can be used to spread lies and rumours about the victim. The narcissist may use their flying monkeys to further isolate them from their support network, by spreading vicious lies and rumours about them. This can make the victim feel as though they have nowhere to turn and that no one believes them. It can also make it more difficult for the victim to leave the abusive relationship.

Another reason why flying monkeys may be loyal to the narcissist is that they may have their own issues with co-dependency or low self-esteem. They may feel as though they need the narcissist's approval or validation, or that they are not strong enough to stand up to them. They may also be afraid of being on the receiving end of the narcissist's abuse if they do not comply with their wishes.

So what can you do if you are the victim of a narcissist's flying monkeys?

To protect yourself, it's crucial to maintain boundaries and refuse to engage with them, as doing so will give the narcissist more power over you. Seek support from trusted friends or family members who understand the situation and can offer a listening ear and emotional support. Additionally, it's essential to work on building your self-esteem and self-worth, as these qualities can serve as a shield against the emotional onslaught of the narcissist and their flying monkeys. Remember, it's not your job to convince others of the truth; focus on healing and taking care of yourself, and the truth will eventually reveal itself.

Triggers

Triggers are external or internal stimuli that remind someone of a traumatic experience, and can cause them to feel overwhelmed or distressed. Understanding what triggers are and how they affect someone is an important step in managing symptoms of trauma.

Here are some key points to help understand triggers:

- Triggers can be anything that reminds someone of a traumatic experience, such as a place, smell, sound or image.

- Triggers can cause someone to feel a range of emotions, such as fear, anger, anxiety or sadness. They can also cause physical reactions, such as increased heart rate, sweating or shaking.

The way someone reacts when they are triggered can vary depending on the individual and their experiences. The most common reactions include avoidance, numbing, dissociation or hyperarousal.

• **Avoidance** involves actively trying to avoid anything that might trigger a traumatic memory. This can cause someone to withdraw from social situations, stop engaging in activities they used to enjoy or avoid certain people or places. Avoidance has the potential to lead to social isolation, depression and anxiety.

• **Numbing** is a response to trauma where a person tries to block out or suppress the emotions associated with a traumatic memory. This can cause someone to feel emotionally disconnected or numb. It's like a mental defence mechanism that helps a person cope with the overwhelming emotions that come with the trauma. When someone is numbing, they are highly likely to engage in unhealthy coping mechanisms such as substance abuse or self-harm. This is because they are trying to find ways to numb themselves further or distract themselves from the emotions they are trying to avoid.

• **Dissociation** involves feeling disconnected from oneself or the world around them. This can cause someone to feel like they are watching themselves from outside of their body, or to have gaps in their memory surrounding a traumatic event. While dissociation is a natural response to trauma, it can also be a symptom of a mental health condition such as dissociative disorders. People with dissociative disorders may experience dissociation as a result of past trauma, but it can also happen in response to other stressful situations. Dissociation will interfere with a person's ability to function normally and as a result will impact their relationships and daily life.

• **Hyperarousal** involves feeling intensely activated or on edge and can cause someone to be easily startled, irritable or anxious. Hyperarousal is a normal response to stress or danger, but it can also be a symptom of a mental health condition such as PTSD. People with PTSD may experience hyperarousal as a result of trauma, even when there is no current danger present. In general, hyperarousal can interfere with a person's ability to function normally. It can make it difficult to concentrate, sleep or relax.

It's important to seek professional help from a healthcare provider or mental health professional if you or someone you know is experiencing triggers. They can help identify the underlying trauma causing the above responses, and find healthier ways of addressing the trauma and dealing with the symptoms. Treatment options may include therapy, medication or a combination of both.

I have known many people use their 'triggers' as an excuse for their behaviour. While sometimes their triggers do cause them to behave in ways that aren't deemed acceptable, some triggers that are experienced are in fact a warning from your gut instinct that something isn't right, and these warnings should not be ignored.

Are you triggered or ignoring your gut instinct?

Alex was a freelance consultant who did very well for herself; there was nothing she particularly wanted, and she had everything she needed. She was a victim of narcissistic abuse and had been single for four years after that relationship ended to work on healing her triggers and building herself back up again. She had met a new partner, James, who openly admitted to having some mental health issues and was fairly insecure. Alex knew what it was like to suffer from mental health issues, so she could relate to so many things he was experiencing. Alex saw so much good in James she decided to look past those issues and began a relationship with him. After eight months James moved in with Alex, he was working a part-time job which he did in the evenings so he couldn't contribute much towards the bills. But Alex was okay with this, she didn't want to pressure James, and he did say that he would pull his weight around the house to compensate for not being able to contribute so much towards the bills.

As time went on, Alex noticed that James would find ways to get out of paying for things, making up excuses so that she would end up paying. He would also show a keen interest in how much her contracts were pulling in. He often asked her about her finances and would make comments about how well she was doing and how that made him feel small. These comments and questions made Alex feel very uncomfortable; she would often lie about how much she earned in an attempt to make James feel better about himself. James also stopped helping around the house claiming that his depression was getting too much. Yet he would always have the enthusiasm to go to the gym every day.

This went on for a couple of months before it got to the point where she could no longer handle James's constant questions, so she decided to ask why he was no longer able to make any contributions. James's reaction was completely unexpected and caused Alex to break down. James accused her of being secretive and unsupportive, saying that she did not want to create a life with him. He said she needed to deal with her triggers so that she stopped behaving in this way which was causing major problems in their relationship. Alex thought long and hard about how James reacted and what he had said to her. Yes, she had responded to his outburst by becoming emotional, but she remembered how she felt having that pit in her stomach every time James would mention her finances. She had a feeling that something was wrong and sharing the truth with him could be a problem. Every time she would ignore this feeling, convincing herself that she was being silly.

After some reflection, Alex realised that she had not made any significant changes to her behaviour, but James had changed and failed to follow through on his commitments. Whenever Alex expressed her concerns, James would deflect the blame onto her, claiming that her reactions were triggered by her unresolved issues, instead of acknowledging his own hurtful behaviour. When Alex finally decided to end the relationship and asked James to leave, she saw his true colours. James revealed himself to be a narcissist, likely a covert one, who had been deceiving and manipulating her from the beginning. Alex discovered that he had been seeing another woman while living with her, confirming that her reactions to him were not due to her own unresolved triggers, but rather her intuition warning her that something was off. In hindsight, Alex realised she should have trusted her gut and ended the relationship sooner.

In the next chapter I talk about going *no contact* which you will notice helps you begin to heal your triggers.

12

How to Handle a Partner with a Big Ego

Your ego is your sense of self-importance or self-esteem.

When kept within sane limits, a healthy ego is necessary for a relationship to work because you need to have a healthy sense of self-esteem to be in a healthy relationship. Partners can have a tendency to 'peacock' in the early stages of a relationship. Many see this as a red flag, thinking it is narcissistic and is something to be concerned about.

Peacocking doesn't always mean a person is a narcissist, it likely means they just want to impress you. Yes, you could confuse this type of behaviour with someone who is a narcissist, but this only becomes narcissistic when your partner uses the 'peacocking' to define their status with an expectation of admiration, along with some of the other traits listed in Chapter 3 – and remember they need to show a clear and consistent pattern of those behaviours for there to be a concern.

When your partner has a big ego, you will notice that they have a desire to be right at all times. This desire also means that they pay little attention to your feelings or what it is you want. Remember that in a relationship you should have an equal say with your opinions being respected. Often a compromise is needed and it is important that you express this to your partner.

Partners with big egos struggle with communication, this will make your attempts to express yourself difficult. What you will find is that your partner turns the relationship around to make it all about 'you' as you always want to bring up things which you feel need addressing and they don't want to face it.

When your partner displays a lot of arrogance, this is a sign that you're in a relationship with someone who has a big ego. Your partner feels they are better than you because they earn more, are more successful in their career or it could be the result of some abstract factors they have put together in their mind. Remind yourself of what it is about your partner that drew you to them in the first place. Do they still have those wonderful qualities and is their new-found arrogance due to a change in circumstances? This is a conversion that you need to have with them – and yourself!

Sometimes people just need reminding of their reality. If your partner truly loves you, they will respect you for bringing this to their attention. But maybe you are at a point where you have decided that it is time to end the relationship. You have tried communicating to fix things and your partner is being difficult, not giving you the space that you need to be able to let go and move on.

Grey rocking before no contact

When it comes to ending a relationship with a partner who has a big ego, the best course of action is often to go *no contact.* However, this can be a difficult step for many people to take, especially if they are not yet ready to cut ties completely. In these cases, a strategy known as *grey rocking* can be a useful starting point. But this strategy does come with a warning as it can also agitate that person and lead them to create more drama and conflict. This is not necessarily a strategy that I would advise you to use on someone who has violent tendencies and is quick to fly into a rage. Also, if you have children with this person, grey rocking can have a negative effect on your relationship with your child. When a parent chooses to grey rock the narcissistic ex, this can look odd to the child, and the narcissist may use this to exploit the situation painting you as the problem to your child.

So how does grey rocking work?

By channelling a grey, boring rock, becoming flat, as uninteresting as possible and equally showing no interest in them, there is a chance that they will begin to lose interest, which is the goal! This is because those with narcissism always want a reaction, even a negative one is a reaction that will keep their egos boosted.

Here are some tips on how to grey rock a partner:

- **Keep your responses short and neutral**. When communicating with your partner, try to keep your responses brief and to the point. Do not share any personal information or express your emotions with them, as this may give them an opportunity to engage with you.

- **Limit your interactions.** Try to reduce the amount of time you spend with your partner, and limit your interactions with them as much as possible. This will help to create a sense of emotional distance between you and your partner.

- **Avoid discussing your personal life.** Avoid sharing details about your personal life, interests or feelings with your partner. This will make it difficult for them to engage with you and give you the space you need to disengage.

- **Be polite but uninterested.** When interacting with your partner, maintain a polite and respectful tone, but keep your interactions short and uninterested. This will signal to them that you are not interested in engaging with them on a deeper level.

- **Don't engage in arguments**. If your partner tries to engage you in an argument or conflict, do not take the bait. Stay calm and neutral, and refuse to engage in any verbal sparring or confrontation.

Although grey rocking is a good strategy, it is not a guarantee that your partner will disengage from the relationship. Seeking support from friends, family, at this time will help you to navigate the process. The next step, and it is a healthy step, is to go no contact.

What is NO CONTACT?

Firstly, understand that this is a very different technique to what a narcissist uses when they want to block and ghost someone (as I explained in Chapter 4).

When you decide that it is time for you to remove that person from your life and go no contact it is because you no longer want to be treated badly by them. This is a sign that you are starting to respect yourself and understand your worth. This means big changes are going to come as a result of you going no contact. Going no contact sends a clear message not only to the person you are removing but also to yourself!

Here is an ordered list of steps for successfully going no contact:

- **Decide to go no contact:** The first step is to make the decision to go no contact. Making this decision means there is no going back! This means cutting off all communication and contact with the person who is causing you to be upset.

- **Set boundaries:** Once you've made the decision to go no contact, set clear boundaries for yourself. This means deciding that it is time to work on yourself and you will no longer give any more of your time to the other person.

- **Prepare for possible reactions:** Going no contact may provoke a strong reaction from the other person. Prepare yourself for this possibility by anticipating their response, and having a plan in place to defend yourself and not give them a reaction back, because yes you will still maintain no contact.

- **Remove reminders:** In order to successfully go no contact, it's important to remove any reminders of the other person from your life. This will include unfollowing and blocking them on social media, blocking and deleting their phone number, deleting all of your pictures of them, pictures of you and them together and initially avoiding places where you may run into them.

- **Build a support system:** Going no contact can be difficult, and it's important to have a support system in place to help you through it. Tell those close to you what your plans are moving forward, and that you will be needing their support during this time. Often exes will reach out to your friends and family to try and get back in touch. Explain your reasons why you needed to go no contact and ask them not to engage with your ex.

- **Focus on self-care:** Going no contact can be emotionally taxing, so it's important to prioritise self-care during this time. This may include getting enough sleep, eating well, exercising and practising relaxation techniques such as meditation. I also highly recommend having a 'full' diary so you have things to look forward to.

- **Stay committed:** Going no contact may be challenging at times, but it's important to stay committed to your decision. Write down the reasons why you made the decision to go no contact in the first place and focus on the positive changes it's bringing to your life. The times you feel as though you are struggling to follow through you can read back your reasons to reaffirm your decision.

- **Seek professional help if needed:** If you're struggling to go no contact, or if you're experiencing emotional distress as a result of the process, consider seeking professional help. A therapist can provide you with support and guidance as you navigate this difficult time. Many who pay to get help often feel indebted to follow through.

13
How to Handle Narcissistic Families

"Blood is thicker than water and you should stand by your family no matter what."

"Family is not an important thing, family is everything."

How many times in your life have you heard these statements? And I'm sure when you have respectful, compassionate and trustworthy family members then maybe these statements are true. But the truth is very different when you have a narcissist in your family.

Narcissistic family dynamics can often be complex, confusing, and will certainly be emotionally damaging for the victim. Narcissistic parents, siblings, or other family members can create an environment of manipulation, abuse and control that can leave the victim feeling lost, helpless and deeply wounded. In this chapter, we will explore the dynamics of narcissistic families.

Understanding narcissistic families

A narcissistic family is one in which the needs, wants and desires of the narcissistic parent(s) are prioritised over those of the children. The narcissistic parent(s) may be overt or covert in their behaviour, but the underlying motivation is the same: to maintain power and control over their children. The following are some common characteristics of narcissistic families:

- **Lack of empathy:** Narcissistic parents are unable to empathise with their children's needs or emotions. They often dismiss or minimise their children's feelings, telling them they are "overreacting" or "being too sensitive."

- **Emotional manipulation:** Narcissistic parents will use emotional manipulation to control their children. They may guilt-trip, shame or blame their children for their own shortcomings, creating a sense of obligation and indebtedness.

- **Gaslighting:** Narcissistic parents will use gaslighting techniques to make their children doubt their own perceptions and reality. They will deny events or conversations that took place or twist them to suit their own agenda.

- **Enmeshment:** Narcissistic parents will create an environment of enmeshment, where boundaries between parent and child are blurred or non-existent. They often treat their children as extensions of themselves, rather than as individuals with their own identities.

- **Triangulation:** Narcissistic parents will use triangulation to pit their children against each other, or to create alliances that serve their own purposes. They often withhold affection or attention from one child while favouring another, creating competition and resentment.

- **Emotional neglect:** Narcissistic parents may be emotionally neglectful, failing to provide their children with the love, support and nurturing they need to thrive. They will prioritise their own needs over their children's, leaving them feeling ignored or unimportant.

Becki was raised in a narcissistic family dynamic. She had a narcissistic mother, a younger half-sister and a step-father who she could never seem to connect with despite her attempts to. Her mother would demonstrate all of the above behaviours, and she felt very isolated, like she was the black sheep of the family, which is a very common feeling when you are raised in a narcissistic environment.

Becki's mother showed a huge dislike to everyone around her and made claims that no one could be trusted – only she could be trusted, yet Becki never felt that was the case. In public Becki's mother would take great pleasure in frequently embarrassing her, or telling people what a difficult child she was. Her mother would always quickly follow up that statement with how she was struggling to cope, but was doing her best, basking in the sympathy and attention she would receive as a result of that lie.

Becki was naturally a shy child and she lacked confidence, with the belief that no one could be trusted she struggled to speak up and make connections with others. Often Becki would cling to just one person, as she would feel overwhelmed and intimidated in a group of people. This behaviour carried on into her early adulthood, a deep fear of not being accepted.

She was physically abused on a regular basis by her mother until she got to an age where Becki had stopped reacting to the abuse, so her step-father would take over. Becki's step-father was like a puppet, he would do exactly what his wife told him to do including beating Becki when her mother wasn't feeling in control of her daughter's thoughts and behaviours. He was very much controlled by his wife, as with all narcissists they need to be in control of everyone around them.

Becki didn't have a relationship with her half-sister because of the triangulation that her mother used. Many times, Becki would find that her belongings would be taken without her permission (stolen) and used by her sister. When she tried to get them back, her mother would fly into a rage claiming that she was the problem and that she should learn to share and not be so selfish. This left Becki feeling confused, she was raised believing that stealing wasn't right, and then when her half-sister stole from her, she was being told that it was right. Every time Becki would bring this to her mother's attention, she would be physically reprimanded. As a result, she became very shut down, she would avoid talking to her parents and half-sister, because the times she did try to communicate with them she seemed to become a problem, and she was often bullied about her looks and weight. So Becki found herself spending most of her time in her room.

Becki never received any affection, but would frequently see her sibling receive it. This lack of affection led her to believe that she was unlovable, and she was confused as to why this was the case, as all she ever wanted was to be accepted and to have a relationship with her mother. This feeling of rejection translates into a belief of 'not being good enough', a common thought pattern that can lead to a variety of behaviours and patterns in adulthood.

One of the most common behaviours is self-doubt and low self-esteem. Victims will struggle with feelings of inadequacy and as a result they may constantly seek validation and approval from others, they will also likely be highly sensitive to criticism or rejection.

Another common behaviour for a child who has developed this belief is self-sabotage. As an adult that person may engage in behaviours that undermine their own success, such as procrastinating or avoiding tasks that could lead to positive outcomes. They may also struggle with setting boundaries and saying no to others, which can lead to burnout and resentment.

In some cases, a person who has experienced narcissistic abuse as a child may also develop narcissistic traits themselves. This can happen as a way to protect themselves from further abuse, or as a result of internalising the narcissistic behaviours they experienced.

It's important to note that everyone's experience is unique, and there is no one "right" way to behave after experiencing narcissistic abuse. However, seeking therapy or counselling can be helpful in processing past trauma and developing healthy coping mechanisms.

Narcissistic siblings

Dealing with narcissistic siblings can be an extremely difficult and draining experience. Unlike relationships with friends or romantic partners, we are born into families and are lead to believe that we have to maintain contact with our siblings, regardless of the challenges we may face. When one or more of those siblings exhibit narcissistic traits, it can create a toxic and unhealthy dynamic that can leave lasting emotional scars.

One of the most challenging aspects of dealing with narcissistic siblings is their sense of entitlement and lack of empathy. Narcissistic individuals hold a belief that they are entitled to special treatment or attention. This can create an unhealthy dynamic within the family, where the narcissistic sibling demands constant attention or praise, and may become resentful or even hostile if they don't receive it.

Another challenge of dealing with narcissistic siblings is their tendency to engage in manipulative and controlling behaviour. Narcissistic individuals often try to control others through various tactics, such as guilt-tripping, gaslighting or playing the victim. They may also use triangulation in an attempt to create conflict between family members, or to turn family members against each other.

Dealing with a narcissistic sibling can also take a toll on your own mental health and emotional well-being. It's common for family members of narcissistic individuals to experience anxiety, depression and even PTSD as a result of the emotional abuse they endure. This can lead to feelings of isolation and loneliness, as well as a sense of being trapped in an unhealthy dynamic that seems impossible to escape. However, there are ways to cope with narcissistic siblings and to protect your own mental health and well-being. One important step is to establish healthy boundaries with your sibling. This may involve setting limits on the amount of time you spend with them, or the topics you discuss with them. It may also involve speaking up when you feel uncomfortable or disrespected by their behaviour.

Another key step in dealing with narcissistic siblings is to seek support from others. This may involve confiding in a trusted friend or family member, or seeking out a therapist who specialises in family dynamics and narcissistic abuse. Talking about your experiences and feelings with others can help to validate your experiences and provide a sense of relief and healing.

It's also important to recognise that you are not responsible for your narcissistic sibling's behaviour. While it can be tempting to try to fix or change them, ultimately, it's up to them to take responsibility for their actions and seek help if needed. Your role is to protect your own mental health and well-being, and to set boundaries that allow you to maintain a healthy relationship with them (if possible) without sacrificing your own needs or values.

Family or not, any environment or person that is toxic should be recognised as such. Know that it is okay to go no contact with them, especially if they have failed to accept your boundaries and continue to treat you in a way that amplifies your mental health issues as a result of their behaviour.

How to handle narcissistic family members

As you are aware, narcissists live their lives in patterns. In order for you to be able to create a reasonable relationship with the narcissist you must first identify their patterns. Knowing these will help you create a plan on how to navigate the narcissistic family dynamic in the best way possible. The truth is when you are dealing with narcissistic family members, it is likely to always be a challenge, but there are some strategies that can be implemented to help you manage the situation more effectively. Here are some possible tips and examples:

- **Limit your time:** Don't feel obligated to turn up to and spend every family event with the narcissistic family member. Set yourself a 'time' boundary which could look like the following:

    1. Only seeing them on events such as birthdays and Christmases.

2. Limit the amount of time you spend at the event, i.e., two hours maximum.
3. Have a genuine reason ready why you can't spend so much time with them. Have plans to do something else which requires you to split your time accordingly.

- **Communicate your needs and limits clearly and assertively:** Once you have identified the narcissist's patterns, learn to speak up so that you can take yourself out of the toxic behaviour pattern. For example, "I appreciate that you want to spend time with me, but I need some space right now. Let's talk later." There is a possibility that your request won't be accepted by the narcissist, so you do have the option to make it clear that you will block them until you are ready to give them your time once again.

- **Avoid triggers:** The narcissist will have various triggers, so it is important you identify the topics, situations or behaviours that tend to trigger the narcissistic behaviour. For example, politics: "I know that discussing politics with you always leads to arguments, so let's agree to disagree and focus on something else." Don't allow yourself to get caught up in their need to always be right.

- **Don't take it personally:** Recognise that the narcissistic behaviour is not about you, but about the other person's own issues and insecurities. If you have triggered the narcissist, don't allow yourself to be gaslighted by them. Instead explain that you understand that you're feeling upset, but you didn't mean to offend them. Then offer to find a solution together to balance out the situation.

- **Seek support:** Build a network of people who can offer you emotional support, validation and perspective. This can be with other family members who can see the narcissistic behaviour, or friends who would be willing to listen to you when you are struggling with your family's behaviour, and you could use someone to talk to.

Communication is key when dealing with a narcissist.

"It is impossible to argue with someone who believes their own lies."

There are many types of communication tools that are recommended and can be used when dealing with a narcissist, such as grey rocking and no contact. But depending on the victim's circumstances there is no 'right' way to communicate, and when you have a big family dynamic it is about finding a way that is going to be the healthiest for you. Studies have shown that no contact gives the best results, allowing the victim to heal in the quickest way possible. Many do feel guilty when they go no contact, and this feeling of guilt is emblematic of the trauma bond, making them feel responsible for the abusers' hurt. Those who have children with a narcissist tend to go no contact after the children have reached adulthood.

No contact does have limitations for those who are not yet in a position to execute this style so they will opt for low contact instead, which is a tight style of communication where you learn to communicate with no emotion and only when necessary. When going low contact there is no casual communication, for example, asking how their day is going. The only time you communicate is when there is an event, such as a funeral or a hospital admission that requires it.

Yellow rocking however is a powerful technique that can help you cope with narcissistic family members in a way that is both effective and compassionate. The term "yellow rocking" was coined by Shahida Arabi, a bestselling author and expert in narcissistic abuse recovery.

The basic idea behind yellow rocking is to adopt a neutral and non-reactive stance when interacting with a narcissistic family member. Instead of getting drawn into their drama or trying to change their behaviour, you simply observe and acknowledge what they are saying or doing, while remaining centred and grounded in your own sense of self.

Here are some examples of how to execute yellow rocking with a family member:

- **Stay calm and focussed:** When a narcissistic family member is trying to provoke you or push your buttons, take a deep breath and remind yourself that their behaviour is not about you. Focus on your own thoughts and feelings, and try to stay centred in the present moment.

- **Use minimal responses:** Instead of engaging in a lengthy argument or trying to explain yourself, use short and simple responses that acknowledge what the other person is saying without adding fuel to the fire. For example, you could say "I hear what you're saying" or "I understand your point of view" without agreeing or disagreeing.

- **Don't take the bait:** Narcissistic family members may try to bait you into an argument or manipulate you with guilt or shame. Recognise these tactics and don't take the bait. You can simply say "I'm not comfortable discussing this right now" or "I need to take a break from this conversation."

- **Practise self-care:** Yellow rocking can be emotionally draining as it goes against your natural communication style and requires effort, so it's important to take care of yourself before, during and after interactions with narcissistic family members. Make sure to engage in activities that nourish and replenish you, such as exercise, meditation or spending time with supportive friends or family members.

Yellow rocking is a great way to deal with narcissistic family members because it allows you to maintain your own sense of self and boundaries, while still acknowledging the other person's perspective. It's a way of communicating that is non-judgemental, non-reactive and empathetic, which can help defuse conflicts and promote healing in relationships.

14
How to Handle a Friend with a Big Ego

We can all relate to having one or two friends who always seem to be out for themselves. Those types of friends who:

- Want plans to revolve around them.
- Have a problem with not always being invited.
- Feel the need to talk about others negatively.

Ultimately, they are selfish, appearing more focussed on their own needs and desires than those of others. It's also important to note that everyone can be selfish at times, it's normal human behaviour. It's only when this behaviour becomes excessive and persistent and starts to affect relationships, that it might be considered a problem. It's important to approach these 'selfish' situations with empathy and understanding and try to understand the reasons behind the behaviour.

Let's say you have a friend who is successful, and always boasts about their accomplishments and puts others down. They constantly interrupt conversations to talk about their own achievements and dismiss others' ideas and opinions. Here are some key points on how you can deal with this person:

- Acknowledge and validate your friend's accomplishments, but also acknowledge the accomplishments of others. This shows that you are listening to them but also not letting them dominate the conversation.

- Encourage your friend to ask questions and listen to others. This will help them to develop empathy and understand other people's perspectives.

- Help your friend to understand that their behaviour is not helping them to build strong relationships. Explain that people will be more likely to listen to them and value their opinions if they are respectful and considerate of others.

- Encourage your friend to practise humility and self-awareness. Remind them that being aware of one's own ego and being able to control it, is a sign of maturity and strength.

- Provide your friend with positive feedback when they show humility and listen to others. This will reinforce the behaviour you want to see.

It is important to remember that people with big egos often have a deep-seated insecurity or fear, and this behaviour is a way for them to cope with these feelings. By handling the situation with empathy and understanding, you can help your friend to become more self-aware and ultimately, a better person.

What about jealous friends?

Having a jealous friend can cause significant problems in your friendship and affect others involved in the relationship. Jealousy is an emotion that is linked to insecurity, envy and a lack of trust. When your friend displays jealousy, it can create an uncomfortable and awkward dynamic within the friendship that is difficult to navigate. It can also damage the trust and closeness that healthy friendships require. For instance, if your friend becomes jealous of your accomplishments or successes, they may try to undermine or belittle you instead of congratulating you. This creates a competitive atmosphere within the friendship, which is not conducive to healthy relationships.

Apart from causing issues within your friendship, a jealous friend can also negatively impact your other relationships. If your friend becomes jealous of your other friends or romantic partner, they may try to interfere or create drama. This can lead to tension and conflict, and may even cause other people to distance themselves from you.

Jealousy is a natural emotion, but when it becomes a recurring pattern of behaviour, it may be a sign of deeper psychological issues like narcissism. If your friend exhibits jealous behaviour consistently, it may be necessary to talk to them honestly about how their behaviour is affecting the friendship. In some cases, you may have to distance yourself from the friendship if their behaviour continues to be a problem.

Your friend may experience jealousy for a range of psychological reasons, such as insecurity, envy, fear of abandonment, unresolved past issues or personality traits. If your friend acknowledges their tendency towards jealousy, it can create significant challenges in maintaining a healthy friendship. By understanding the reasons behind their behaviour, you may be able to work together to overcome these issues and build a stronger friendship.

15

How to Handle Big Egos at Work

We spend so much of our lives working we would like to think we can find a job which provides us with a good level of satisfaction, and appreciation from those we work with and for. However, the reality of finding your dream job, with a dream employer and equally amazing colleagues isn't what we always end up with.

When you happen to be working with a colleague or a boss who has a big ego, they have the ability to make your life a complete misery and turn your dream job into a nightmare!

Those with big egos in a professional environment are very unpleasant to work with and often show signs of *the dark triad.* The three pillars/traits of the dark triad (DT) are;

- **Narcissism**
- **Machiavellianism**
- **Psychopathy**

These three traits that form the dark triad can be present at both subclinical and clinical levels.

When traits are referred to as subclinical, this means that the level of a trait or behaviour that is being presented is not severe enough to meet the diagnostic criteria for a clinical disorder, but the traits or behaviours that are being shown are still noticeable and are likely to be problematic in many areas of their lives.

Even at lower levels, certain personality traits will still cause distress, interfere with relationships or job performance and lead to negative consequences. For example, let's say someone has a subclinical level of neuroticism. This means they experience some level of anxiety or worry, but it is not severe enough to be diagnosed as an anxiety disorder. Similarly, someone with a subclinical level of impulsivity might be more likely to act impulsively than the average person, but not to the extent it significantly impairs their ability to function in daily life.

Whilst these three traits (narcissism, Machiavellianism and psychopathy) are not always presented to the clinical level of a mental disorder like NPD or APD, an individual who is showing these behaviours or traits will still cause numerous issues in the workplace and prove to be very difficult to work with. All of these traits that form the dark triad are characterised by having no empathy and have distinctive manipulation styles.

When it comes to identifying if your colleague or boss has a dark personality, it can sometimes be difficult. Recognising any of these signs in your work colleague doesn't automatically make them someone who has the dark triad. For someone to have this, they need to show a consistent pattern of behaviour which clearly demonstrates these three personality traits.

Only a qualified clinician can make a diagnosis, it is important to bear this in mind when reading through this book.

While there are many different types of narcissists, how narcissism shows up in the workplace is often observed in two types. Your overt narcissist has a strong sense of entitlement, a high need for power and an arrogant and condescending attitude. Those who seem to fall into the covert category, will appear very differently to your overt type of narcissist. They will frequently put others down in order to make themselves look better than those they work with. They may also make inappropriate comments as a way to get noticed.

The covert narcissist will regularly claim that they never get treated fairly, and this is because they believe that many others who they work with are actually jealous of them, and don't want them to do well. This constant need for attention that a narcissist requires can feel very draining in the work environment. Management is essential here to prevent other members of staff from becoming sucked into the narcissistic vortex!

When someone who is high in narcissism is faced with criticism in the workplace, or needs to deal with a negative report or feedback, they will discard all that is presented to them. This happens even when the evidence has come from a reliable source; the narcissist will quickly use their manipulation skills to devalue and discredit the source. For example, suggesting the employee is lying and will then confidently come up with a different version of the story. The narcissist will likely claim that they themselves have over-contributed to the company, and should be respected and recognised for this, and that listening to idol gossip from others is ridiculous.

The way a narcissist uses manipulation in the workplace is to protect their ego! If a colleague has been given a promotion, someone who has the dark triad is likely to respond in one of these ways:

• **Minimising the promotion:** Individuals with dark triad traits may try to downplay the significance of the promotion, claiming that the job isn't as good as it seems and suggesting that they have insider information to back up this claim.

• **Devaluing the person:** Another tactic of the dark triad is to devalue the person who got the job, claiming that they don't have the capacity to cope with the new role and suggesting that they will eventually burn out and not be able to keep the job.

• **Taking credit:** In some cases, individuals with dark triad traits may claim they helped the person get the job and that it's all thanks to their input and support. This behaviour is an attempt to bolster their own status and importance, even if it comes at the expense of others.

Machiavellianism in the workplace

Machiavellianism is a term used to describe individuals who are focussed on their own interests and use a certain manipulation style to gain political power. The word itself comes from the Italian philosopher Niccolò Machiavelli, who was a 16th century renaissance diplomat and author. Machiavelli believed that using deceitful, immoral, and cruel behaviours was necessary to maintain political power. He wrote *The Prince*, a piece of literature which encourages politicians to act in unsavoury ways to gain and maintain their power.

Individuals who score high in Machiavellianism tend to be great candidates for complex job roles. They are goal-oriented, have good impulse control and exceptional long-term strategic planning skills. However, because their manipulation style can be so subtle, detecting this trait can be challenging.

Machiavellians are masters of impression management techniques, giving them the ability to influence others to maximise opportunities for their own personal power. They are deceitful and have a calculating interpersonal style. Although they claim they can be trusted, they have a cynical view of human nature and appear not to trust anyone.

Unlike a narcissist or psychopath who desperately wants acknowledgement, individuals with Machiavellianism have no interest in fame. Instead, they work behind the scenes using someone who has power as a puppet to orchestrate their grand plans. They keep important information to themselves for their own use and will never share it with colleagues to help the organisation reach its goals.

Machiavellians are opportunists! They see a colleague's promotion as an opportunity for themselves, asking the question, "How can this promotion be helpful to me?" They openly encourage others to lie and use coercive persuasion to serve their own needs.

When a complaint is made, a Machiavellian will make the person believe that the complaint will be taken seriously and acted upon. But the reality is that complaints would not be followed up, especially if they felt that information could be useful to them at a later date.

In summary, Machiavellianism is a trait that allows individuals to manipulate others for their own personal gain. They have a cynical view of human nature, are deceitful and have a calculating interpersonal style. They are excellent long-term planners, but their manipulation style can be challenging to detect.

Psychopathy in the workplace

Psychopathy is often regarded as the most sinister of the dark triad traits. Individuals with this trait exhibit pathological lying and a complete lack of guilt or remorse. They are deceptive and fearless in their manipulative personal style, intentionally making things personal to achieve their goals.

Psychopaths use bullying tactics to encourage employees to develop a personal relationship with them, which diverts their attention from their job responsibilities and instils a sense of loyalty to the psychopath. This, in turn, makes the psychopath feel powerful. Individuals with psychopathy have no qualms about violating morals. They make quick, impulsive decisions that prioritise short-term goals and disregard long-term consequences. They derive pleasure from seeing others suffer and enjoy creating chaos within their teams or staff. They often cause organisational disruption by constantly questioning authority figures and challenging existing rules and policies. Although questioning authority and rules can be constructive, psychopaths do it solely to undermine the functioning of the company and they derive pleasure from this.

Psychopaths are also adept at causing others to fail. They appear encouraging, pushing their colleagues to make risky decisions quickly. This is because they derive pleasure from seeing others make mistakes and get into trouble. They use this tactic when they dislike someone and want to get rid of them or when a colleague poses a threat that needs to be eliminated.

Additionally, psychopaths have poor listening skills. They appear uninterested in others' stories, especially if the story is emotionally charged. They present fake smiles and glance around the room, avoiding eye contact. They may even think about their response while the other person is speaking, rather than truly engaging with them.

Research has shown that psychopathy is prevalent in some workplaces, particularly in positions of power. Psychopaths can have a profound negative impact on the workplace, leading to reduced morale and productivity, high turnover rates and legal issues. It's crucial for employers to identify and address psychopathic behaviour to ensure a healthy and productive work environment.

Summary of how Dark Triad (DT) individuals can impact others in the workplace:

• **Manipulative interpersonal style:** DT individuals have a manipulative interpersonal style that can make others feel uncomfortable or uneasy. They often use charm, flattery and deception to influence others to do their bidding. This can create a toxic work environment as other employees may feel like they can't trust their co-workers or managers.

• **Undermining co-workers:** Undermining their co-workers in order to gain more power or control. For example, they may spread rumours or engage in gossip to damage their co-workers' reputations. They may also take credit for their co-workers' ideas or work or try to sabotage their co-workers' projects or initiatives.

• **Bullying and intimidation:** Individuals with high levels of DT traits may engage in bullying or intimidation tactics to get what they want. They may use fear or threats to force others to comply with their wishes, or engage in aggressive behaviour to assert their dominance. This can create a hostile work environment and lead to high levels of stress and anxiety for other employees.

- **Lack of empathy:** Those who have any of the DT triads will lack empathy for others, which can make them seem cold, calculating and uncaring. They may be willing to sacrifice the well-being of others in order to achieve their own goals or objectives. This can create tension and conflict within the workplace, as other employees may feel like they are not being treated fairly or with respect.

- **High turnover rates:** DT individuals will create a workplace environment that is toxic, stressful or unpleasant, which can lead to high levels of employee turnover. This can be costly for the organisation, as it can lead to a loss of institutional knowledge and require significant resources to recruit and train new employees.

- **Lack of team spirit:** DT individuals may be more focussed on their own interests than on the interests of the team or the organisation as a whole. They may be unwilling to collaborate or compromise with others, which can hinder the team's ability to work effectively together. This can create a sense of division and competition among colleagues, which can be detrimental to team morale and productivity.

- **Lack of accountability:** DT individuals may refuse to take responsibility for their mistakes or shortcomings. They may blame others for their failures or try to cover up their mistakes. This can create a culture of blame-shifting and can make it difficult for colleagues to trust them.

- **Exploitation:** DT individuals love to exploit others for their own gain, whether it be for financial gain or to boost their ego. They may take credit for other people's work, use their colleagues to achieve their own goals, or exploit their power to get what they want. This can be detrimental to team morale and can create a sense of resentment and distrust among colleagues.

How to deal with a toxic colleague

One of the biggest difficulties when working with a dark triad individual is dealing with their supporters. Those with the dark triad often have a backup of other work colleagues that support and sometimes encourage their bad behaviour. So, raising your issues with a superior might not be a worthwhile thing to do. This is because the colleague with the big ego is likely to have the skills to twist the situation in their favour and get *let off the hook*. At the same time, this makes you of course appear to be the 'bad' one. That doesn't mean that you should suffer in silence, and I know many would say 'Just leave your job if they are that bad' but that also isn't going to give you the answer.

Chances are you'll enter a new job and meet yet another colleague who has a big ego.

Evidence is what is going to support you when it comes to dealing with that difficult colleague. Your emotions will be stirred when you're around this person with the focus being on what they are saying, or often what they are not saying! And how they are behaving to get everyone else around them to become avid followers. Thinking clearly will become difficult for you, so it is time to get organised.

Set up a specific folder to hold all of your evidence when you have dealings with this person. Accept the fact you have a second job, and that is to document all of the communication between the two of you. This documentation is crucial when it comes to dealing with someone who has a big ego, as often they 'forget' what they said. Also include anyone else in the folder who seems to be 'in' on the bad behaviour.

When you have meetings or communicate with this person, always make sure you have a witness in the room with you. No matter how awkward it may seem to ask, to have someone join you in a one-to-one meeting, this is an important part of the process. You do have the right to say that you don't feel comfortable alone in that person's presence, it is important to make that clear. Sometimes this request alone is enough to get that person to think about their actions/behaviours when you are dealing with them in the future.

Typing up minutes after meetings and emailing them to the difficult individual with your superior cc'd in and whoever else was in on that meeting, with a request for confirmation that the email was received and they agree with the context of it, will save you a lot of 'mis-communications' and 'mis-understandings' in the long run.

This will not always be welcomed by that difficult person, but it is necessary to carry this out to protect yourself in the future, making it clear that you value clarity.

There are ways you can manage and prevent damage caused by those with the dark triad in the workplace.

One of the biggest mistakes an organisation can make is giving a few people a lot of power. There is a correlation with those who are in powerful positions and those who have higher dark triad traits. Many organisations believe that giving people more power will yield better results, but this is not always the case. This thinking can also create a 'group' of people who will run the company based on fear.

Power allows people to act in accordance with their internal traits, the more power someone has, the more we see who they truly are – their true trait expression. By having a team of individuals who have high dark triad traits you will end up with a dysfunctional company, fearful, unhappy employees and likely a lawsuit!

It is important for organisations to create an ethical work environment. It is always a good sign when an organisation's values are to follow ethics. Those with the dark triad won't be accepting of this, so likely won't take the job or last long working for a company who encourages employees to follow their values. Moral reasoning is highly affected by the environment, companies that encourage this will have a diverse team that will bring about positive changes, encouraging ethical discussion making processes that will benefit the organisation in the long term.

If you think you have someone with the dark triad working for you – DO not promote them!

If you think you have interviewed someone with the dark triad – DO not employ them!

If you think you work with someone who has the dark triad, follow the procedure listed above to protect yourself, minimising their impact on you.

Here is a process that you can use deal with a toxic colleague:

1. **Set boundaries:** Clearly communicate your expectations and what you are comfortable with in terms of behaviour and communication. Work on your confidence when it comes to delivering how you will and won't be spoken to.

2. **Focus on facts:** When dealing with a dark triad individual, it's important to stay calm and avoid getting drawn into arguments or emotional reactions. Instead, focus on facts and specific examples of their behaviour. You almost need to become an emotionless 'parrot' that doesn't sway from the facts and is only interested in getting the matter at hand resolved.

3. **Avoid confrontation:** Dark triad individuals can become defensive and aggressive when confronted. Instead, try to address the issue in a calm and non-threatening way, and try to avoid

situations where confrontation is likely. If the person you work with does have a tendency to become defensive and aggressive, it is particularly important to ensure you always have someone with you during the times you need to communicate with them.

4. **Document everything:** Keep a record of any incidents or exchanges with the colleague, including dates, times and what was said. This can be helpful if you need to escalate the issue to a manager or HR. It is important that you show clarity, and have all the facts listed in order, in an easy-to-read fashion.

5. **Seek help from a trusted manager or HR representative:** If the situation becomes difficult to handle, it may be necessary to bring it to the attention of a manager or HR representative that you trust. They may be able to offer additional support or help to resolve the situation.

It's important to remember that dark triad individuals often have a hard time understanding how their behaviour affects others, and expecting them to change is often futile. It's better to protect yourself and focus on how to manage the situation with the above process.

What would be the easiest way for an organisation to deal with a difficult employee who is showing dark triad traits?

The truth is, there isn't an easy way!

Why companies struggle to sack employees: when the dark triad works against you

Sacking a toxic employee would seem like the best route. However, one of the biggest reasons companies struggle to sack employees with the dark triad, is the legal and practical considerations involved. Many companies fear being sued for wrongful termination or discrimination if they attempt to fire a difficult employee. They are right to fear this, because something that a narcissist loves to do is go to court!

Even before there is a sniff of a lawsuit, they will make it clear that if you don't play ball with them, and follow 'their' rules then court will be where they will see you next. They have no shame in making that very clear.

You see, when there is potential for legal action to take place, a narcissist will see this as a challenge and an opportunity to show off their power and of course their ability to win!

Employees who have the dark triad are difficult, as these people are skilled at concealing their true nature. Companies may need to gather extensive evidence and documentation to support their case, which can be time-consuming and costly.

In some cases, companies may also fear retaliation from employees with the dark triad, who may be prone to revenge-seeking behaviours or even violence. This can create a sense of fear and uncertainty in the whole workplace, making it difficult for managers and colleagues to take action.

The second biggest reason is that dark triads are usually found at the top!

This factor is what can make it difficult for victims to have their stories taken seriously when there is a prevalence of dark triad individuals at the top of organisations. Research has shown that narcissistic and psychopathic traits are more common among CEOs and other high-level executives than in the general population. This can create a culture of normalisation and acceptance of these traits within the organisation, making it difficult for employees who are targeted or harmed by colleagues with the dark triad to have their experiences taken seriously. It can also make it more difficult for companies to take action against these individuals, who may be seen as valuable or indispensable to the organisation.

If you find yourself working for an organisation that is filled with dark triad individuals who are making your life hell, then I hate to say it, but it's time to hand in your resignation. When you are working for a team of dark triads who are treating you badly there is nothing you can do to make your life easier, other than saying goodbye! Your mental and emotional health will thank you for that decision to leave in the long run!

Now let's take a look at how to develop your mental and emotional health in the next chapter.

16

Emotional Intelligence: the Game Changer

Not many know what emotional intelligence is. Often people think it is related to your level of IQ (Intelligence Quotient), but that is a completely different set of skills. Our IQ is concerned with verbal, spatial, visual and mathematical skills. Ultimately it gauges how we learn new things, can focus on tasks, retain and recall objective information and manipulate numbers.

The correct term for Emotional Intelligence is Emotional Quotient, EQ for short.

There are different EQ scales that are taught and used in various settings, including education, workplace and personal development. Here are some of the most common EQ scales:

- **Mayer-Salovey-Caruso Emotional Intelligence Test (MSCEIT):** This is a performance-based test that measures emotional intelligence using four branches: perceiving emotions, using emotions, understanding emotions and managing emotions.

- **Bar-On Emotional Quotient Inventory (EQ-i):** This is a self-report measure that assesses emotional and social functioning across five composite scales: self-perception, self-expression, interpersonal, decision making and stress management.

- **Emotional and Social Competence Inventory (ESCI):** This is a 360-degree assessment tool that evaluates emotional intelligence across four domains: self-awareness, self-management, social awareness and relationship management.

- **Trait Emotional Intelligence Questionnaire (TEIQue):** This is a self-report measure that assesses emotional intelligence across fifteen facets, including emotion perception, emotion regulation, empathy and social skills.

- **Emotional Intelligence Appraisal:** This is a self-assessment tool that measures emotional intelligence across four domains: self-awareness, self-management, social awareness and relationship management.

Each of these EQ scales has its own unique approach to measuring emotional intelligence, and they may vary in terms of their format, administration and interpretation. Ultimately, the choice of which EQ scale to use will depend on the specific goals, context and population being assessed. Emotional intelligence is a multifaceted construct that encompasses a range of skills and abilities related to perceiving, using, understanding and managing emotions effectively. Each of these EQ scales assesses different aspects of emotional intelligence and can provide valuable information on an individual's strengths and areas for improvement.

With my method I suggest practical exercises and techniques to enhance emotional self-awareness, emotion regulation, empathy and social skills, thus helping you to reflectively regulate your emotions in a way that promotes emotional and intellectual growth. You will have a great capacity to objectively assess your strengths, be open to viewing and challenging your limitations, mistaken assumptions, unacknowledged biases and short-sighted beliefs.

Being high in EQ also gives you the ability to read political and social environments, and landscape them in a way that gives results, thus remaining unfazed in stressful situations and being engaging, becoming the kind of person others want to be around.

Those of you who have spent time with a narcissist know what it's like to be in stressful situations (that they create), feeling like your emotions are out of control, your ability to express yourself seems lost and somehow slowly but surely your mind becomes more confused. This is of course as a result of the gaslighting and abuse, and you then end up questioning if you are the one who's the problem.

Self-awareness and self-regulation are the first set of skills that are looked at on the EQ scale. These initial skills are what will help you to become unfazed by any gaslighting, so then you'll be in a position to stop that narcissist in their tracks!

Becoming a master with each step in the EQ scale won't just help you repel narcissists.

It will also allow you to grow, becoming confident in all areas of your life.

This is the order in which I recommend you learn how to develop your emotional intelligence:

Self-Perception/Awareness

Self-Expression

Interpersonal

Decision Making

Stress Management

Developing a high level of emotional intelligence is the key to your success in life. And when I say success what I am actually saying is happiness!

By developing each competency, you will not only accelerate the healing process from all the trauma that you've experienced, but you will also prevent yourself from getting sucked in by another person who has a toxic ego in the future. When you have a high level of emotional intelligence, you are more likely to make healthy decisions, build healthy relationships and achieve your goals. So, take the time to develop your emotional intelligence, and watch as your life transforms into one of confidence, success and happiness.

Self-perception

Becoming self-aware is the process of understanding yourself. So many are disconnected with themselves, this is especially true when someone has been subjected to abuse. This realm of emotional intelligence concerns what many generally refer to as our 'inner self'.

The competencies associated with self-perception are:

- Emotional Self-awareness: Understanding your emotions and their impact on your life.
- Self-regard: Respecting and accepting your strengths and weaknesses.
- Self-actualisation: knowing your self-worth and capabilities.

Increasing your self-awareness is by far one of the most important parts of your recovery when you've been in a toxic dynamic with a narcissist. Many lose their identity when they have been in this type of relationship. Self-awareness is the starting point to not only getting back the person you once were, but also becoming a stronger, more resilient version. When you have a high level of self-awareness you have the ability to build strong relationships and communicate more effectively.

Self-awareness is about recognising and understanding your emotions – what you're feeling and why, and understanding what you think and do as a result. Whenever you have had a relationship with a narcissist, in any dynamic, you would have been subjected to emotional abuse. This means your emotions will be dysfunctional, and you'll be experiencing a lot of confusion as a result.

When you have a high level of self-awareness you have the ability to listen and trust your intuition. This helps you to instinctively make good decisions that will impact all aspects of your life.

When you've been in a relationship with a narcissist you are made to believe that you are incapable of making good decisions. And, of course, the unhappy relationship you've chosen to stay in would confirm that you can't make good decisions. This is another reason so many struggle to get out – because they can't trust themselves to make good decisions.

When you develop your self-awareness, you become acutely aware of your strengths and weaknesses and what is important to you. Your values and moral compass become a part of who you are, and these core beliefs help you to navigate your way through the world in a confident manner.

Many believe that by reflecting on why we are the way we are (using introspection) is what will improve our self-awareness. By examining the causes of our own thoughts, feelings and behaviours this will give us enough insight into where we need to make changes. This is a great starting point, but this will not work on its own when you've experienced narcissistic abuse.

The mind is designed to think, and your subconscious stores everything!

By going inwards, you are asking your mind to unlock hidden traumas and for you to assess/make sense of them without further guidance. This can be very damaging and can set you back.

Self-awareness isn't something that you achieve once and then you're done with it. Every moment in life gives you an opportunity to either be self-aware or not. It is a continual endeavour, a conscious choice to be self-aware.

The good news is that the more you practise it, the easier it becomes, and eventually it becomes second nature.

Having a high level of self-awareness makes it impossible for your emotions to rule you!

Success in this area means that you are aware of your feelings, you feel strong, and have confidence when it comes to pursuing life's goals.

Self-expression

Once you've mastered self-perception, you'll be able to tune into your emotional expression. Managing your emotions – particularly the ones that are perceived as 'negative' emotions – is crucial if you're to face up to big egos in the future!

The competencies associated with self-expression are:

- Emotional Expression: Ability to express your feelings verbally and non-verbally
- Independence: Self-directed and free from emotional dependency on others
- Assertiveness: Ability to express yourself in a non-destructive way

Understand that all of your emotions are valid. There is no such thing as a negative emotion as many of us are taught to believe. When you have been in a relationship with a narcissist you will become very reactive. This isn't due to the fact you are an aggressive person, instead it is because you have been triggered. When your needs and emotions are suppressed for such a long time, there is a need to be heard that builds up inside of you. When that frustration has reached boiling point, the next emotion to show itself is anger.

When you experience this emotional outburst, you will feel completely out of control. This is what we call 'reactive abuse'; it's an expected response from the abuse you've been subjected to. Being in a toxic relationship will alter your ability to think clearly. Instead, you become reactive from dysfunctional emotions. Practise being calm: step back and take a deep breath.

Remind yourself how important it is to stay true to your values, and hold yourself personally accountable for any mistakes. Regardless of what you went through, it is important that you always treat others with respect. Once you learn how to self-regulate, you will no longer experience these uncomfortable emotional outbursts. You will be in control of your life and reactive abuse will become a thing of the past.

Codependency and independence stand as opposites. By developing your independence competency, you actively counteract codependent traits, paving the way for the cultivation of healthier patterns in your relationships with others.

Understanding codependency

It is common for codependants and narcissists to be in a relationship because of how they enable and compliment each other's behaviours.

Codependency is a pattern of behaviour where individuals excessively rely on others for their sense of self-worth, identity and emotional stability. It often stems from dysfunctional family dynamics, trauma and a lack of healthy boundaries. Codependent individuals will prioritise others' needs and desires over their own, leading to a loss of personal autonomy and a distorted sense of self. Codependency manifests in various ways, such as enabling destructive behaviours, seeking validation from others and experiencing anxiety or guilt when attempting to assert personal boundaries. This is why people who are trapped in codependent patterns often find themselves in one-sided (often narcissistic) relationships, where their self-esteem is contingent upon the approval and validation of their partner.

Embracing independence

In contrast to codependency, interdependency embodies a healthy and balanced approach to relationships. Interdependent individuals recognise their inherent worth and value their autonomy, while also acknowledging the importance of connection and collaboration. They maintain a strong sense of self and willingly engage in mutually-beneficial relationships, where both parties contribute to each other's growth and well-being.

When you develop your independence, it boosts your emotional intelligence by fostering healthy communication, setting boundaries and cultivating empathy. It encourages individuals to express their needs and desires while respecting the autonomy and boundaries of others. In interdependent relationships, there is a genuine sense of support, trust and interconnectivity, where both parties are equal contributors.

Developing and embracing your independence should not be underestimated!

Losing your voice and being unable to express yourself in a toxic relationship is a common occurrence. It is expected and not unusual. However, developing assertiveness can empower you to communicate confidently and effectively. By cultivating assertiveness, especially after enduring a toxic relationship that silenced your voice, you open up a path to personal growth and healing. Assertiveness lies between passive and aggressive communication styles, striking a healthy balance. It entails expressing your thoughts, feelings, needs and boundaries clearly, respectfully and without causing harm. Mastering this skill is crucial for building and maintaining healthy relationships.

Interpersonal

Once you have a solid understanding and confidence in who you are, and in your abilities to express yourself without needing validation from others, the next step is being able to confidently build relationships, and I am not just referring to intimate ones, I am talking about all of life's relationships.

The competencies associated with interpersonal are:

- **Relationships:** Develop and maintain healthy relationships
- **Empathy:** Recognise, understand and appreciate the feelings of others
- **Social Responsibility:** Ability to contribute to society, social groups and to the welfare of others, in other words, kindness

By developing and honing these competencies, you will acquire the ability to foster and sustain gratifying relationships characterised by a balanced exchange of giving and receiving. These relationships will be distinguished by open expressions of trust and compassion, be it through verbal communication or observable behaviours. In our pursuit of happiness and contentment, relationships hold immense significance as they directly influence our overall well-being. The quality of our connections with family, friends, romantic partners and colleagues profoundly impacts our satisfaction in life.

Achieving and maintaining fulfilling relationships necessitates a delicate equilibrium of various skills. Social responsibility entails recognising and considering the impact of our words, actions and choices on others and the world around us. By embracing social responsibility, we acknowledge our role in fostering a positive and supportive environment for ourselves and those we interact with. This concept forms the bedrock for constructing healthy and gratifying relationships. Kindness, a seemingly uncomplicated yet profoundly impactful act, possesses the ability to generate ripples of positivity in our relationships. When we approach others with kindness, we demonstrate compassion, understanding and generosity. Kindness nurtures trust, strengthens connections and fosters a sense of belonging. By embracing the diverse ways in which kindness can be expressed, whether through spoken words or tangible gestures, we have the power to transform our relationships into nurturing and enriching bonds.

The decision-making realm

This is one of the most exciting realms of emotional intelligence as you now get the opportunity to use your emotions in the best way to solve any problems that come up whilst making optimal choices. Your ability to deal with situations that once seemed too daunting or difficult, now become an opportunity for success. Your confidence when it comes to making great decisions will become second nature.

The competencies that are associated with decision making are:

- **Impulse control:** Ability to resist an impulse to react
- **Reality testing:** Being present, remaining objective by seeing things as they are
- **Problem solving:** Solving problems where emotions are involved

Many believe that this area of EQ is only useful when applied in work situations. This will absolutely be valuable when you are dealing with a colleague or boss who has a big ego, but when you master these elements in the EQ scale, you will also be able to remove any feelings of guilt and shame, thus being able to control certain emotions that push you towards acting irrationally.

Levels of impulsivity intensify when we don't have the awareness required to keep our emotions in check, and that is when our stress management skills become void. Often in the aftermath of a toxic relationship, the ability to maintain your self-control is at a very low level, and if you have been subjected to gaslighting, then you will struggle to remain present and think clearly enough to solve any problems that arise.

Impulse control is having the ability to resist impulsive reactions and maintain your self-control. This is a crucial aspect of developing effective decision-making skills. Impulse control involves being able to manage your emotions and thoughts, resisting the urge to react in a knee-jerk way and taking the time to consider the consequences of your actions. It is essential to learn how to control impulsive behaviour in order to make clear-headed decisions so that it can help you move forward positively after a toxic relationship.

Developing impulse control involves a variety of strategies, such as practising mindfulness, meditation or deep breathing exercises. When you're feeling overwhelmed or triggered, taking a step back and focussing on your breathing can help you maintain emotional balance and resist the urge to react impulsively. Additionally, setting clear boundaries with yourself and others can help you maintain self-control and make better decisions that align with your values and goals.

Reality testing can only work when you are able to be present and are thinking objectively when making sound decisions. Reality testing involves being able to see things as they are and not as you wish they were. This means that you need to be honest with yourself and evaluate situations and people objectively, without allowing emotions or biases to cloud your judgement. This is incredibly difficult for many people to do which is why so many end up trapped in a toxic relationship. To develop this skill, you need to be able to practise self-reflection and self-awareness. You need to have the patience to examine your emotions and thoughts, and question any biases or assumptions you may be holding on to. It's also important to seek feedback from others, especially those you trust and who have your best interests at heart. Feedback can help you gain an objective perspective and see things from a different point of view, which can be useful when making important decisions.

Solving problems when emotions are involved is difficult, but it is another critical component of decision making. In the aftermath of a toxic relationship, it's common to feel overwhelmed and unsure about how to move forward. Being able to solve problems effectively can help you develop a plan of action and move forward in a positive direction.

Effective problem solving involves a variety of skills, including the ability to identify and define the problem, gather information and resources, generate and evaluate potential solutions and implement and monitor the chosen solution. One of the best ways to develop this skill is through practice. By breaking down problems into smaller, more manageable parts and working through them systematically, you can develop the confidence and skills needed to make better decisions in the future.

Stress management

It's inevitable that we will face various stresses and challenges throughout our lives, and of course when you're dealing with someone who has a big ego, you will find it very challenging and stressful. This part of emotional intelligence is key when it comes to 'coping'.

The competencies associated with stress management are:

- **Flexibility:** Ability to adapt your feelings, thinking and behaviour to change
- **Stress tolerance:** Ability to cope with stressful or difficult situations
- **Optimism:** Ability to remain hopeful and resilient, despite setbacks

Stress is a natural response to challenging or threatening situations. However, when stress becomes chronic, it can have a significant impact on our physical, mental and emotional well-being. When we're in a toxic relationship, we will be subjected to ongoing stress and anxiety due to the unhealthy dynamics and negative interactions with that person.

To heal and recover from toxic relationships, we need to develop competencies that help us manage stress effectively. These competencies include flexibility, stress tolerance and optimism.

Flexibility is the ability to adapt our feelings, thinking and behaviour to change. When we're in a toxic relationship, we may become rigid in our thinking and behaviour as a way of protecting ourselves from further harm. However, this rigidity can prevent us from moving forward and finding new, healthier relationships. By developing flexibility, we can learn to adapt to new situations and people, allowing us to move on from the toxic relationship and find healthier relationships.

Here are some tips and exercises that can do to help develop flexibility:

1. **Practise mindfulness:** Mindfulness can help you become more aware of your thoughts and feelings in the present moment. By practising mindfulness regularly, you can learn to observe your thoughts and emotions without judgement, and be more flexible in your response to them.

2. **Challenge your assumptions:** Many of us have deep-seated beliefs and assumptions that can limit our ability to be flexible. To challenge these assumptions, try questioning them and looking for evidence that contradicts them. This can help you see things from different perspectives and be more open to change.

3. **Try new things:** One way to develop flexibility is to step outside your comfort zone and try new things. This could be something as simple as trying a new food or taking a different route to work. By exposing yourself to new experiences, you can become more adaptable and better able to handle change.

4. **Practise problem solving:** When faced with a problem or challenge, open up your mind to all possibilities with a flexible mindset. Instead of getting stuck on one solution, try to brainstorm multiple solutions and be open to trying different approaches.

5. **Learn to let go:** Sometimes, being flexible means letting go of things that are no longer serving you. This could be a job, a relationship or a belief that no longer aligns with your values. By learning to let go of what no longer serves you, you can create space for new opportunities and experiences.

6. **Embrace change:** Change is inevitable and learning to embrace it can help you develop flexibility. Instead of resisting change, try to approach it with curiosity and openness. This can help you see change as an opportunity for growth and learning.

Stress tolerance is the ability to cope with stressful or difficult situations. When we're in a toxic relationship, we are likely to experience ongoing stress and anxiety due to the negative dynamics and interactions with our partner. To heal and recover, we need to develop the ability to cope with this stress effectively. The first step in this process is acceptance, then you can learn new coping strategies, such as meditation, exercise or therapy, that help us manage our stress and anxiety.

Here are some tips and exercises that you can do to help build your stress intolerance:

1. **Identify your triggers:** Knowing what triggers your stress response can help you to avoid or manage stressful situations more effectively. Take some time to reflect on what situations, people or events cause you to feel stressed or anxious. Once you identify your triggers, you can work on developing coping strategies to manage them.

2. **Build a support system:** Surrounding yourself with supportive people who understand what you are going through

can be incredibly helpful. Reach out to friends, family or a therapist who can offer you emotional support and guidance. Be sure to seek out people who lift you up and avoid those who bring you down.

3. **Practise self-care:** Taking care of yourself physically, emotionally and mentally can help you to build resilience and cope with stress more effectively. This can include things like getting enough sleep, eating a healthy diet, exercising regularly and engaging in activities you enjoy.

4. **Challenge negative thoughts:** Negative self-talk and limiting beliefs can increase stress and anxiety. Try to challenge negative thoughts by asking yourself if they are really true, and if there is evidence to support them. You can also try replacing negative thoughts with more positive and empowering ones.

5. **Learn to relax:** Relaxation techniques, such as deep breathing, progressive muscle relaxation or visualisation, can help you to calm your mind and body when you are feeling stressed or anxious.

6. **Set realistic goals:** Setting realistic goals can help you to avoid feeling overwhelmed and stressed. Break down large goals into smaller, more manageable steps, and celebrate your progress along the way.

Optimism is the ability to remain hopeful and resilient, despite setbacks. When we're in a toxic relationship, we may feel hopeless and trapped, with little hope for the future. However, by developing optimism, we can begin to see the potential for positive change and growth in our lives. This can help us stay motivated and focussed on our goals, even when faced with challenges or setbacks.

Here are some tips and exercises that can do to help develop your optimism:

1. **Reframe negative thoughts:** One of the most effective ways to develop optimism is to challenge negative thoughts and reframe them in a more positive light. For example, instead of thinking "I'm never going to find someone who loves me" try thinking "I am worthy of love and will find someone who appreciates me".

2. **Practise gratitude:** Focussing on what you are thankful for can help to shift your perspective to a more positive outlook. Make a habit of writing down three things you are grateful for each day and regularly expressing appreciation to others.

3. **Visualise success:** Visualisation is a powerful tool that can help you to achieve your goals and maintain a positive outlook. Spend time visualising yourself achieving your goals and experiencing positive outcomes.

4. **Take care of your physical health:** Taking care of your physical health can also help to boost your mood and increase feelings of optimism. Exercise regularly, eat a healthy diet and get enough sleep.

5. **Learn from past experiences:** Reflect on what you have learned from your past experiences, both positive and negative. Use those lessons to inform your future choices and maintain a hopeful outlook.

6. **Practise self-compassion:** Finally, it's important to be kind and compassionate to yourself. Recognise that setbacks and challenges are a natural part of life and treat yourself with the same kindness and compassion you would show to a friend.

Together, these three competencies work to help us manage stress effectively, allowing us to heal and recover by developing flexibility, stress tolerance and optimism.

Once we start to work on these we can begin to move forward in our lives, finding new, healthier relationships and building a brighter future.

17

How to Deal with a Narcissist – Once and for All

The truth is when it comes to dealing with a narcissist it starts with you. And I am not saying that it is now time for you to forgive the narcissist, or that you need to take full responsibility for what happened to you. No, not at all!

You don't need to forgive anyone who isn't willing to accept the role that they played in your trauma. These people do not deserve your forgiveness. What you experienced, and what happened to you was a result of the narcissist's abusive behaviour.

Understanding the way a narcissist works, the tactics they use, and being able to link those tactics to your experience and how that has affected you, is key in your recovery.

Narcissists have one goal in life and that is to win at all costs. In their eyes, winning confirms their stature and high position in society which means that no matter what you do or what script you are following, you can't ever win.

As you have made your way through these chapters you may have come to realise that no matter what subtype you are dealing with, they all 'function' with the same set of traits.

And I believe that a narcissist will fluctuate between all of these subtypes, rather than being fixed in that category. This can be due to a variety of factors, including changes in the individual's environment, stress levels or interpersonal relationships, as well as fluctuations in their mood or self-image. For example, a narcissist who is experiencing a period of success and adulation may exhibit more grandiose and entitled behaviour, while one who is feeling insecure or threatened may display more aggressive or defensive behaviour, like a malignant narcissist. Additionally, some narcissists may shift between different subtypes depending on their goals or the situation at hand, such as switching from a charming, seductive persona to a more controlling or manipulative one in order to maintain power or influence over others.

Ultimately, while narcissistic individuals will exhibit common traits and behaviours, their complex personalities and individual circumstances can lead to a range of different subtypes and fluctuations in their behaviour over time.

Something that a narcissist doesn't want you to know, and that I want you to understand, is that inside every narcissist there is a truly broken, unconfident, insecure person who never wants to be exposed for who they truly are. But this doesn't mean you should feel sorry for them. We all have the ability to change, and without knowing we often make small changes each and every single day. When it comes to making changes, we need self-awareness. In other words, we need to be able to look deep inside ourselves, observe our behaviours and learn new ways to better them.

Even for a normal, healthy person this is a difficult thing to do. So can you imagine how difficult this would be for a narcissist who has created an identity which they show to the world as someone who exudes nothing but power and self-assurance, to then look at their flaws and set about making a change. And covert narcissists relish in the attention that they receive as a result of all the lies they have created around their victim persona.

The power of being high in emotional intelligence should not be underestimated. When you have the ability to recognise and manage your own emotions, as well as recognising others' emotions, you will have a strong sense of self, knowing who you are and how others affect you on multiple levels. You will be confident in handling yourself in all situations with a confident communication style. Narcissists will struggle to manipulate you and gain any level of control over you.

I believe that there are as many as one in ten people who are narcissistic, so your chances of meeting someone with a big ego is high. Narcissism will never disappear, although I would like to think that with more awareness and with opportunities to get help in suppressing and changing the toxic traits, it can certainly be something that is manageable.

Boundaries are an important aspect of self-care and healthy relationships

Boundaries allow you to communicate your needs and expectations clearly; they are limits or guidelines that you set for yourself in order to establish and maintain healthy relationships. Boundaries can be physical, emotional, intellectual, spiritual, or sexual in nature. They are important for promoting self-care, self-respect and healthy interactions with others. Without boundaries, you may struggle to communicate your needs, regularly feel like you are being taken advantage of, and experience emotional distress.

Setting boundaries can be a challenging process when you have experienced trauma, abuse, or neglect. It can also be difficult for people who have been conditioned to prioritise the needs of others over their own or who have been taught that setting boundaries is selfish or rude. However, setting boundaries is a critical aspect of self-care and is essential for maintaining healthy relationships with others.

There are several steps you can take to set boundaries effectively. The first step is to identify the specific behaviours or actions that are problematic or uncomfortable. This might include behaviours such as interrupting, criticising or invading personal space. Once the problematic behaviours have been identified, you can then communicate your boundaries clearly and assertively. This might involve saying something like,

"I feel uncomfortable when you interrupt me during conversations. Please allow me to finish speaking before responding."

Another important aspect of setting boundaries is enforcing them consistently. This means that when someone violates a boundary, you need to communicate your discomfort or dissatisfaction and reinforce the boundary. For example, if someone continues to interrupt despite being asked to stop, you may need to remind them of the boundary and disengage from the conversation if necessary.

Narcissists are individuals who have an inflated sense of self-importance, they struggle with empathy, humility and the ability to see things from other people's perspectives.

Narcissists struggle to accept boundaries because they view them as a threat to their sense of superiority and entitlement. The reason narcissists have difficulty respecting other people's boundaries is because they are often preoccupied with their own needs and desires. Sometimes, narcissists will view boundaries as a challenge to their control and dominance. They may become defensive or aggressive when confronted with boundaries and may try to undermine or invalidate the other person's needs or feelings.

In order to set boundaries with narcissists, you need to be clear, consistent and assertive.

You need to communicate your boundaries in a calm and confident manner and be prepared to enforce them when necessary. This may involve disengaging from conversations or interactions that violate your boundaries and setting limits on the amount of time or energy you are willing to devote to the relationship.

Just so you are aware, if you are successful with setting and reinforcing your boundaries with a narcissist, there is a high probability that you'll never hear from them again.

Here are some examples of different types of boundaries:

Physical Boundaries:

- Not allowing others to touch you without your permission, including hugs, handshakes or other forms of physical contact.
- Setting limits on the physical space you share with others, such as not allowing others to enter your bedroom or personal workspace without your permission.
- Setting limits on the amount of physical labour you are willing to perform for others, such as not always being the person who is expected to carry heavy objects or perform physically-demanding tasks.
- Not allowing others to use physical force or violence against you, and being willing to seek help or take legal action if necessary.

Emotional Boundaries:

- Not allowing others to manipulate or guilt-trip you into doing things you don't want to do.
- Setting limits on the amount of emotional labour you are willing to perform for others, such as not always being the person that friends or family come to for support.
- Setting boundaries around the types of conversations or topics you are comfortable discussing with others, and not allowing others to pressure you into sharing personal information or experiences.
- Not allowing others to project their emotions onto you, and being willing to disengage from conversations or situations that become emotionally charged or manipulative.

Intellectual Boundaries:

- Not allowing others to dismiss or belittle your ideas or opinions, and standing up for yourself when someone tries to invalidate your thoughts or experiences.
- Setting limits on the amount of intellectual labour you are willing to perform for others, such as not always being the person who is expected to solve problems or come up with solutions.
- Setting boundaries around the amount of time and energy you are willing to dedicate to work or academic pursuits, and prioritising self-care and rest.
- Not allowing others to speak on your behalf or make decisions for you without your input and consent, and advocating for your own needs and desires.

Spiritual Boundaries:

- Setting boundaries around your religious or spiritual practices, such as not allowing others to pressure you into attending religious services or participating in rituals that do not align with your beliefs.
- Not allowing others to invalidate your spiritual beliefs or experiences, and being willing to respectfully disagree with those who hold different beliefs.
- Setting boundaries around the types of media or information you consume, and avoiding content that conflicts with your spiritual beliefs or values.
- Not allowing others to pressure you into participating in activities or events that conflict with your spiritual beliefs or values, and being willing to respectfully decline invitations or opportunities that do not align with your principles.

Sexual Boundaries:

- Not engaging in sexual activities that you are uncomfortable with or do not consent to.
- Setting boundaries around physical intimacy in relationships, such as not engaging in sexual activities until you feel ready and comfortable with your partner.
- Setting boundaries around the use of contraception or protection during sexual activities, and being willing to assert your needs and preferences in sexual relationships.
- Not allowing others to make unwanted sexual advances or engage in sexual activities without your consent, and being willing to seek support or take legal action if necessary.

Take your time to think about what boundaries you want to put in place.

There is always an option to discuss your ideas with someone else, but remember they are not you, so listen and respect their views before you make a decision on what boundaries you want to set.

Values

Our values are the fundamental principles that guide our lives. They shape our beliefs, our decisions and our behaviours. Knowing your values is essential in creating a fulfilling and purposeful life. However, many people don't know what their values are or the importance of identifying them. Most of our core values are created in childhood, which means they may no longer be relevant and helpful to us now. Actually, there is a possibility that the beliefs that were installed into us from childhood may be what's holding us back and keeping us stuck in toxic cycles.

One of the values that I was taught as a child was the value of a woman. I was raised to believe that as a woman getting married, having children and being a stay-at-home mum with those children were what would make me a woman of 'value'. This belief was part of the reason I stayed in a toxic, abusive relationship. It was a belief that didn't serve me and caused me much harm.

Why is it crucial to know your values?

Knowing your values is crucial for many reasons. Here are some of the key reasons why:

- **They guide your decisions:** Our values are the guiding principles that shape our choices and decisions. When we know our values, we are better able to make decisions that align with our beliefs and principles.

- **They give you purpose:** Our values give us a sense of purpose and direction in life. When we know our values, we can set goals and pursue activities that align with our values, making us feel fulfilled and purposeful.

- **They shape our identity:** Our values are an essential part of our identity. When we know our values, we can create a sense of self-awareness and authenticity. Those who know their values show up in the world with them on display like a badge of honour.

- **They help us to connect in relationships:** Knowing our values is crucial when it comes to building healthy relationships with others. Once we can identify shared values, we can build connections based on common beliefs and principles. This is often where many in relationships fail because they have built the relationship based on their common interests instead of values.

There are two key values that a narcissist does not have, and those values are honesty and kindness. These values are imperative for a relationship to stand the test of time, that is because these are the values that build trust in a relationship.

Tips on how to work out and understand your values

When you do the values exercise set out in this book, following the process below will help you to work out and understand your values. Working out your values involves a process of self-discovery and reflection. Here are some tips to get you started:

• **Identify key life experiences:** Think about significant experiences in your life that have impacted you. This could include moments of success, moments of struggle or times of personal growth.

• **Reflect on these experiences:** Consider how these experiences have shaped your beliefs, principles and worldview. Identify the values that are important to you based on these experiences.

• **Consider your goals:** Think about what you want to achieve in life, both personally and professionally. Identify the values that are important to you based on these goals.

• **Use a values list:** Look up a values list in this book and identify the values that resonate with you. The values exercise can help you identify values that you may not have considered before.

• **Revisit and refine:** Revisit your values regularly and refine them as necessary. Our values may change as we grow and develop, so it's essential to ensure they are still relevant and aligned with our beliefs and principles.

Despite the importance of knowing our values, many people don't prioritise this aspect of self-discovery which will be detrimental to their happiness and future relationships.

Some people may be hesitant to identify their values for fear of being judged or rejected by others. But understand that not everyone is designed to have a place in your life and that is okay, you can still respect others even when your values don't align.

Now let's discover your values!

Values exercise

It is time to work out and understand your values.

Take a look through the table on the last page of this book and physically write down all of the values that you feel are related to you. Once you have your list, pick six and then place them in order from one to six. One being the value that you feel most strongly about.

Once you have ordered your values from one to six, I then want you to ask yourself the following questions for each value:

1. How do YOU show your values to the world?
2. How do OTHERS show you they have the same values as you?

Here are some examples:

The value is **Honesty.**

How do I show the world that I value honesty?

I show the world that I value honesty by choosing to speak the truth. Even at times when lying may seem like a good idea, I chose not to lie. I often pause when others ask me questions, and will ask them if they want an honest answer from me, as I understand and respect that not everyone has this value and will appreciate my honesty. I am also honest with myself and recognise when things aren't working out.

How do others show me that they value honesty? – Bullet point format

- Being respectful of others' opinions, even if they differ from my own.
- Honest individuals take responsibility for their actions and own up to their mistakes.
- When someone is transparent about their intentions, follows through via their actions, and stands by their decisions.

The value is **Loyalty.**

How do I show the world that I value Loyalty?

I show the world that I value loyalty by being consistent in my actions and behaviours.

I show deep commitments and dedication to those with whom I have a relationship or friendship. I am always there when people need me, they can count on me to follow through on my promises. Giving time to my friends and family is important, so I make an effort to spend time with them, showing an investment in our friendship.

How do others show me that they value honesty? – Bullet point format

- They can be trusted with personal information, secrets and feelings
- They stand by me during difficult times and offer emotional support and encouragement.
- They treat me with respect, kindness and consideration, even when they disagree with me.
- They keep in touch regularly and they are open and communicative with me.

The value is **Kindness.**

How do I show the world that I value kindness?

I show the world that I value kindness by actively listening when others speak and share their life with me. I am always grateful when someone trusts me and is able to open up to me. I make an effort to respond with kindness and I want to show them I understand what they said. It is important to me that I treat everyone I meet with respect and kindness, regardless of their background or circumstances. I will go out of my way to help others, even if at times it inconveniences me.

How do others show me that they value kindness? – Bullet point format

- They may make an effort to avoid gossip or negative talk about others, and instead focus on positive conversation and uplifting messages.
- They get uncomfortable when someone is talking negatively about someone else, and they do not engage with the conversion.
- They tend to have a calming or soothing presence in stressful or difficult situations, and try to diffuse tension or conflict with kindness.
- They frequently express empathy and compassion towards others, and try to understand their perspective.

Honesty and kindness are values that an individual who has a toxic ego does not have.

These values are imperative for a relationship to stand the test of time, it is these values that build trust in relationships.

Take as long as you need on this exercise.

The more time and effort you put in the more you will get out. If you are not sure what some of the values mean then google them. The more knowledge you have around these values and how others show theirs, the better your ability will be when it comes to creating healthy connections. However, it's important to remember that certain values can mean different things to different people and may manifest in a variety of ways. The best way to understand what someone values is to engage with them in conversations and observe their actions and behaviours over time. When we are talking about finding a potential partner, at least four months is a good starting point to understanding what their values are.

The next step is setting your standards!

Standards

Having standards is crucial in life because they act as a guide in how we interact with ourselves and others. Standards provide a framework of what is acceptable and unacceptable behaviour, values and principles that guide our lives. Without standards, we can quickly become lost and lack direction, leading to a life of unfulfillment and dissatisfaction.

Why having standards is essential

Having standards ties in with implementing your boundaries and expectations that guide our behaviour, actions and decisions. They are a reflection of our values, beliefs, and principles, which serve as a moral compass to help us navigate through life.

Standards are what help us to build healthy relationships with others, whether it is in personal or professional settings. They are also critical in helping us make decisions about our goals and aspirations, ensuring that we are moving towards a fulfilling life that aligns with our values.

Setting standards for yourself

Setting standards for yourself involves understanding your values, beliefs and principles.

Here are some tips to help you set your standards:

- **Identify your values:** Write down what is important to you in life, such as honesty, integrity, respect and trust. Once you have these, learn how you show your values to the world, and in turn how you would recognise someone who has the same values as you.

- **Define your boundaries:** Be clear about what behaviours you find acceptable and unacceptable from others. For example, you may not tolerate lying, cheating or disrespect. Try to go into as much detail as possible when creating your boundaries.

- **Set goals:** Identify what you want to achieve in life, both personally and professionally and set standards that align with those goals.

- **Communicate your standards:** Be clear about your standards with others so that they know how to respect your boundaries and expectations.

What happens when we lose our standards?

Losing our standards can happen when we become too focussed on pleasing others or sacrificing our values to meet someone else's expectations. This is very common when you have been in a relationship with a narcissist who has manipulated and gaslighted you into believing that their behaviour is acceptable. When we lose our standards, we can become lost, confused, and unsure of who we are and what we stand for.

The effects of being in a relationship with a narcissist

Being in a relationship with a narcissist can cause us to lose our standards, as their behaviour can be confusing and manipulative. Narcissists thrive on power and control, the gaslighting and manipulation tactics they use will ensure you doubt yourself and your values. This can cause you to lower your standards, tolerate behaviour that is unacceptable, and lose sight of what is essential in life.

You no longer need to be that person who a narcissist can single out and use when it suits them. You now have the knowledge on how to develop your emotional intelligence, decide on, set and reinforce your boundaries, work out what your core values are so you can set your standards to once again gain full control back over your life!

This book should have given you an insight into all the signs and signals when it comes to recognising someone who is on the narcissistic spectrum and how to deal with them!

Accepting that these types of people walk among us is crucial in our ever-evolving world of narcissists.

Values Table

1. Authenticity
2. Achievement
3. Adventure
4. Authority
5. Balance
6. Beauty
7. Boldness
8. Compassion
9. Challenge
10. Community
11. Competency
12. Contribution
13. Creativity
14. Curiosity
15. Determination
16. Fitness
17. Freedom
18. Fairness
19. Faith
20. Friendships
21. Fun
22. Growth
23. Happiness
24. Honesty
25. Humor
26. Influence
27. Inner Harmony
28. Justice
29. Kindness
30. Knowledge
31. Leadership
32. Learning
33. Love
34. Loyalty
35. Openness
36. Optimism
37. Peace
38. Popularity
39. Recognition
40. Religion
41. Reputation
42. Respect
43. Responsibility
44. Security
45. Self-Respect
46. Service
47. Spirituality
48. Stability
49. Success
50. Status
51. Trustworthiness
52. Wealth
53. Wisdom

References

Studies that provide evidence to suggest a correlation between social media use and narcissism:

Kircaburun, K., & Griffiths, M. D. (2018). Instagram addiction and the Big Five of personality: The mediating role of self-liking. *Journal of Behavioral Addictions*, 7(1), 158-170. doi: 10.1556/2006.7.2018.01

Twenge, J. M., & Campbell, W. K. (2014). The Narcissism Epidemic: Living in the Age of Entitlement. *Journal of Personality and Social Psychology*, 103(3), 512– 527. doi: 10.1037/a0035718.

References that show the impact social media has on children:

Boyd, D., & Ellison, N. (2007). Social network sites: Definition, history, and scholarship. *Journal of Computer-Mediated Communication*, 13(1), 210-230.

Fardouly, J., Diedrichs, P. C., Vartanian, L. R., & Halliwell, E. (2015). Social comparisons on social media: The impact of Facebook on young women's body image concerns and mood. *Body Image*, 13, 38-45.

Moreno, M. A., Egan, K. G., Barek, S., & Ganahl, R. (2015). Parental awareness and monitoring of adolescent online behavior: A qualitative study. *Pediatrics*, 136(1), 137-146.

References genetic and neurological factors that may contribute to the development of narcissism:

Baskin-Sommers, A. R., Krusemark, E. A., & Ronningstam, E. (2014). Empathy in narcissistic personality disorder: From clinical and empirical perspectives. *Personality Disorders: Theory, Research, and Treatment*, 5(3), 323-333.

Cheung, C. K., & Gillebaart, M. (2019). The neuroscience of narcissism. *Neuroscience & Biobehavioral Reviews*, 98, 299-313.

Demers, L. A., Jacobucci, R., & Rocheleau, G. C. (2019). Epigenetics of narcissistic personality disorder: An exploratory study. *Frontiers in Psychology*, 10, 2603.

Raskin, R., & Terry, H. (1988). A principal-components analysis of the Narcissistic Personality Inventory and further evidence of its construct validity. *Journal of Personality and Social Psychology,* 54(5), 890-902.

Vernon, P. A., Villani, V. C., Vickers, L. C., & Harris, J. A. (2011). Genetic and environmental correlations between narcissism and humor styles. *Journal of Personality*, 79(5), 1061-1084.

References that support the claim that narcissistic and psychopathic traits are more common among CEOs and other high-level executives:

Furnham, A., Richards, S. C., & Paulhus, D. L. (2013). The dark triad of personality: A 10 year review. *Social and Personality Psychology Compass*, 7(3), 199-216.

Hogan, R., & Kaiser, R. B. (2005). What we know about leadership. *Review of General Psychology*, 9(2), 169-180.

Jonason, P. K., Slomski, S., & Partyka, J. (2012). The Dark Triad at work: How toxic employees get their way. *Personality and Individual Differences*, 52(3), 449-453.

Kish-Gephart, J. J., Harrison, D. A., & Treviño, L. K. (2010). Bad apples, bad cases, and bad barrels: Meta-analytic evidence about sources of unethical decisions at work. *Journal of Applied Psychology*, 95(1), 1-31.

Paulhus, D. L., & Williams, K. M. (2002). The dark triad of personality: Narcissism, Machiavellianism, and psychopathy. *Journal of Research in Personality*, 36(6), 556-563.

Printed in Great Britain
by Amazon

41536642R00106